Horse
Breeds
of the World

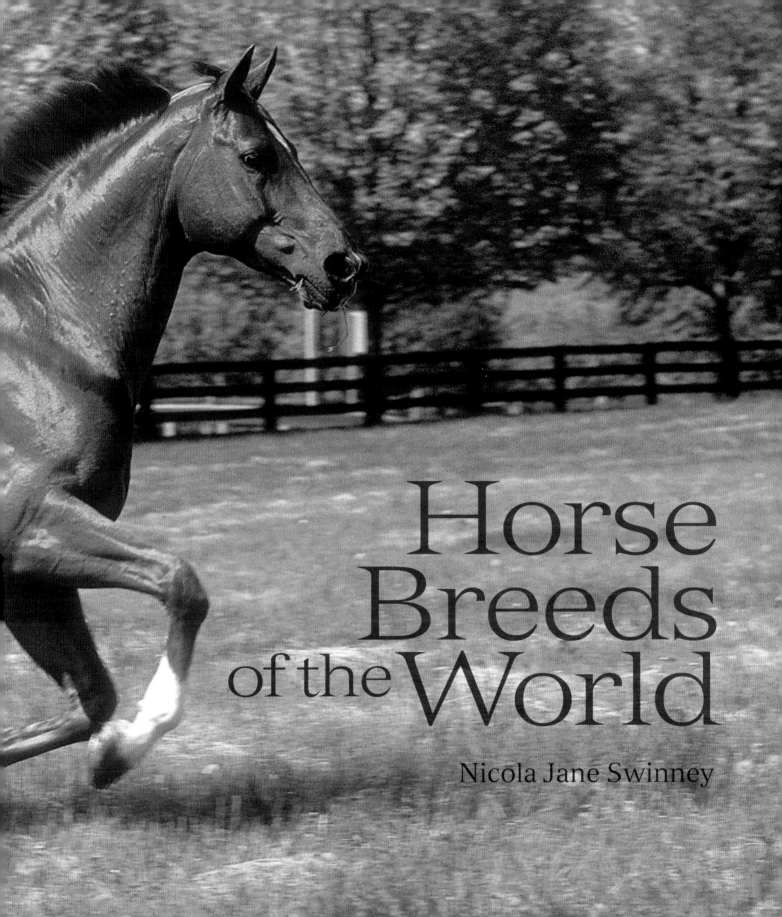

Horse Breeds
of the World

Nicola Jane Swinney

hamlyn

To my parents
Who aren't horsey
But who are wonderful

And to Louis
My most constant companion

First published in Great Britain in 2006 by
Hamlyn, a division of Octopus Publishing Group Ltd
2–4 Heron Quays, London E14 4JP

Copyright © Octopus Publishing Group Ltd 2006

Distributed in the United States and Canada by
Sterling Publishing Co., Inc.
387 Park Avenue South, New York, NY 10016-8810

ISBN-13: 978-0-600-61319-0
ISBN-10: 0-600-61319-4

A CIP catalogue record for this book is available from
the British Library.

Printed and bound in China

10 9 8 7 6 5 4 3 2 1

In this book, unless the information given is specifically for
female horses, horses are referred to throughout as 'he'.
The information is equally applicable to both male and
female horses, unless otherwise specified.

CONTENTS

INTRODUCTION

Horses are people, too. If that sounds a little precious, ask any horse owner. To them, the horse is not simply a mode of transport, a leisure activity or a competition tool – he is their partner, their friend, a member of the family.

So what is it about the horse that so enthrals us? It is hard to believe today, but human beings' first relationship with the equine was that of hunter and prey, to the degree that early horses were hunted almost to the point of extinction. At what stage people experienced that 'eureka' moment, and realized the horse was actually a superb mode of transport rather than just a tasty meal, is not known.

Of course, centuries ago the horse was the *only* mode of transport, and was also vital in warfare. At one time the heavy horse breeds were essential to the warrior, who was so heavily armoured that if he were hoisted on to a pony the unfortunate creature's knees would buckle. As warfare evolved, and weapons changed, a lighter, swifter steed was in demand and the heavier breeds fell out of favour.

In Britain and Europe, the fashionable people about town then wanted flashy, handsome, high-stepping horses to pull their stylish carriages, while wealthy ladies and gentlemen required an elegant mount – the horse as a status symbol. Elsewhere, the horse was still the working man's partner. In agriculture, even the poorest farmer owned a horse, whose role included ploughing the field, carrying the farmer out hunting and pulling the family trap to church. He not only had to be strong and active, and able to survive on fairly meagre rations, but he also had to remain sound.

In the Americas, the horse was vital to both cowboys and Native Americans, the former using him to herd cattle, the latter as a warhorse or simply as transport across the wide open spaces of the Plains. It is probably fair to say that both peoples held their horses in high regard. His speed was vital to them, and it was this that turned him into a leisure industry – horseracing remains a multi-billion dollar business.

It is these changing roles required of the horse that have given rise to the vast diversity of equine breeds we have today, from the graceful Arab – the fairytale drawn by every horse-mad little girl – to the mighty Shire, from Scotland's chunky little Shetland to the striking spotted Pony of the Americas. What almost all modern equines have in common are grace and beauty, coupled with a natural affinity with man and a desire to please.

Horses are some of the best people I know.

Nicola Jane Swinney

Man's early relationship with the first horses was probably that of hunter and prey, although the first equines existed some 60 million years before humans.

The Dawn Horse

The original ancestor of the modern horse is believed to have been *Eohippus*, the Dawn Horse, a small, doglike creature that stood around 35 cm (14 in) tall at the shoulder and who, unlike modern equines, had toes rather than one solid hoof. The skeletal remains of this animal were first discovered in 1841 by Richard Owen, a leading palaentologist who is credited with coining the term 'dinosaur'. Owen believed the creature to be a hyrax – something like a badger – and called him *Hyracotherium*. This animal, in turn, is believed to have derived from a strain of condylarth, which existed 75 million years ago and was the precursor to all hoofed creatures.

There is some debate as to whether the Dawn Horse really was the forerunner to our modern equines – the little creature looked so unlike the horse of today. He had a short snout, rounded back and short legs, with four toes on his forefeet, supported by a pad, and three behind. These pads, similar to those of a dog, still exist in the modern horse as a small, horny callous on the fetlock called the ergot, and would have given his primitive ancestors support on the soft soil found on the forest floors and marshy land. His eyes were set centrally on his head, giving limited lateral vision, and his teeth were short, suited to the consumption of soft, succulent leaves on low shrubs. The Dawn Horse is believed to have existed in what is now North America, which at the time was connected via a land bridge to Asia.

Three-toed horses

Eohippus was followed by *Mesohippus*, a larger mammal with three toes, the central one being most prominent. He still had the rounded back and short head, but his teeth were bigger and stronger, with premolars and incisors, allowing him to chop a greater variety of foliage. The lack of the pads found on the feet of *Mesohippus* suggests his environment was changing from the lush tropical jungle to firmer, drier land and his longer legs would have given him greater speed. *Mesohippus* existed in the Oligocene period, some 35–40 million years ago.

The next evolutions were *Miohippus* and *Merychippus*, both three-toed but slightly bigger and with longer necks. As the teeth of these equine forerunners developed to allow them to chop vegetation, their heads lengthened, their eyes moved further back and to the side of their head, and the arched back lengthened and disappeared.

Towards *Equus*

The first single-toed animal emerged during the Pleistocene period, about ten million years ago. *Pliohippus* had a powerful leg ligament that controlled his single hoof. This small, lightly built creature was the prototype for *Equus caballus* – the latter part of the name means 'of or belonging to horses' – the first true horse.

Pliohippus spread from North America via land bridges to Asia, South America, Europe and finally Africa. As the Ice Age came to an end, these land bridges disappeared, isolating the North American continent and its horses. There is no scientific explanation as to why these horses on their original homeland became extinct, but they are known to have died out about 10,000 years ago, being reintroduced in the 16th century by the Spanish explorers. This is why in this book you will find American breeds listed after breeds from other parts of the world.

Pliohippus was also the basis for zebra and wild asses, and for four distinct types of equid, from which all modern *Equus* have developed. *Equus caballus* had a rigid spine, with short, powerful and well-muscled bones in the upper limbs and long, slender unmuscled lower limbs. He was better equipped for life on the open plain and had a well-developed 'fight or flight' defence system. The foot pad of earlier evolutions became the frog of modern horses' feet.

Primitive man, evolving in Asia, for whom *Equus* was a source of food, followed the horse herds back across the land bridges and was to become the Native American. Human beings' relationship with the horse began some 50,000 years ago when Cro-Magnon hunters, while admiring the creature's beauty, saw him primarily as a meal on the hoof. It would be another estimated 46,000 years before human beings came to regard the horse as a means of transport.

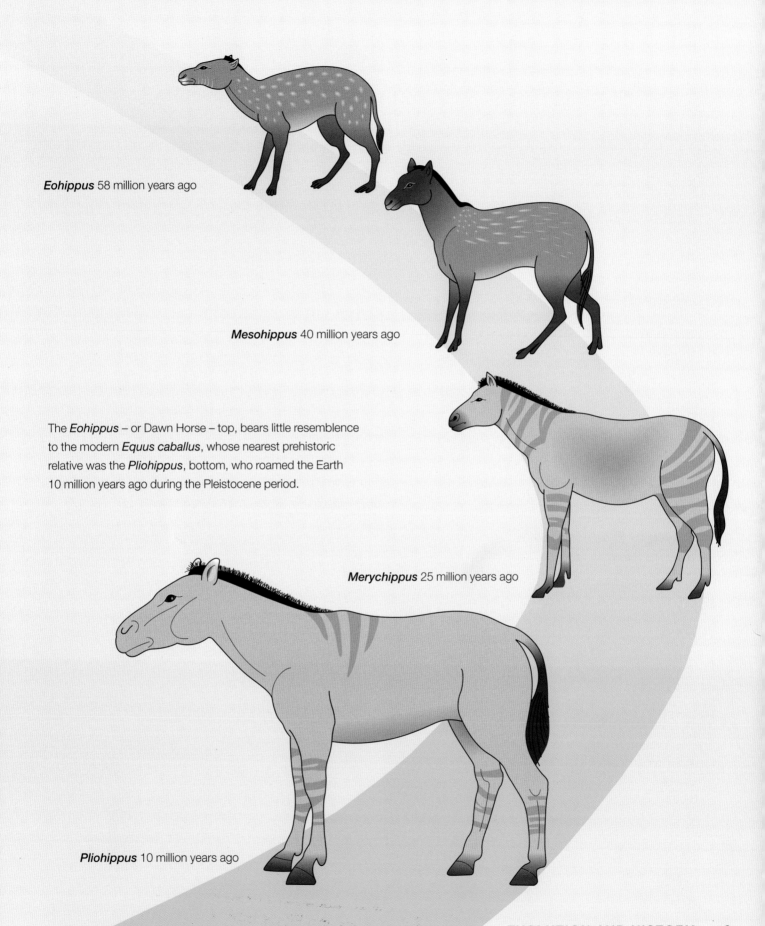

Eohippus 58 million years ago

Mesohippus 40 million years ago

The **Eohippus** – or Dawn Horse – top, bears little resemblence to the modern **Equus caballus**, whose nearest prehistoric relative was the **Pliohippus**, bottom, who roamed the Earth 10 million years ago during the Pleistocene period.

Merychippus 25 million years ago

Pliohippus 10 million years ago

Early horse types

Diluvial Horse

This horse, named for the era in which he existed, was the primitive Forest Horse (*Equus robustus*), from which evolved the coldblooded draught breeds. He was a heavy, thick-legged horse covered in coarse hair, with wide, flat feet suited to the marshy forested land that spread throughout Europe following the Ice Ages.

Przewalski's Horse

Also known as the Asiatic Wild Horse, this is the only truly wild equine still in existence. Hunted by man for meat, he is depicted in cave drawings found in France and Spain that date back some 20,000 years. The horse features heavily in these drawings, so it is probably safe to assume he was found in abundance.

Short and thickset, with erect mane and the 'primitive' dun colouring – with dorsal (backbone) stripe and zebra markings on his legs – the Asiatic Wild Horse was thought to be extinct, until the Russian explorer Colonel Nikolai Mikhailovitch Przewalski rediscovered two small herds living in the Tachin Schara Nuru Mountains near the edge of the Gobi Desert. Since then, and after several abortive attempts, Przewalski's Horse has been reintroduced to the wild. Due to the efforts of the Przewalski Foundation in the Netherlands and breeding preserves in Askania Nova, Ukraine, in 1992 two breeding groups of Przewalski Horses were reintroduced to Mongolia as closely monitored feral herds, with the ultimate plan of reintroducing the animals to the open steppes (plains).

Although Przewalski's Horse is widely believed to be the origin of the modern equine, it should be noted that he has 66 chromosomes, while all other breeds have 64. Furthermore, when bred to a domestic horse, the Przewalski produces fertile offspring with 65 chromosomes.

The Tarpan

Equus caballus gmelini, the Tarpan, was a more lightly built pony type that ranged across eastern Europe and over the Ukrainian steppes, and from which many modern ponies have evolved. The last wild Tarpan, a mare, died in 1880, but the breed has been 'reconstituted' using Przewalski's Horse, Icelandic Ponies, Swedish Gotlands and the Konik (see page 49).

Herds of the Przewalski have been reintroduced. It is the only truly wild equine still in existence.

The Konik – which means 'small horse' in Polish – has been used to reconstitute the Tarpan.

The Tundra Horse

There is some dispute as to whether the Tundra Horse is a distinctly separate type – many believe this wild white pony is an 'offshoot' of the Asiatic Wild Horse. Either way, it has had little influence on modern equines.

Ponies and horses

From these foundations came the four types – two pony and two horse – that form the basis of all existing equines. Pony type 1 inhabited northwest Europe and was a hardy creature, standing about 12.1 hands. His closest modern equivalents are the English Exmoor pony and the Icelandic horse.

Pony type 2 was bigger, up to 14.2 hands, and closely resembled the Asiatic Wild Horse, being mostly dun in colour with the primitive dorsal or eel stripe. He is thought to have been influenced by the Forest Horse, and today's Highland pony, Norwegian Fjord and, to a lesser degree, the Noriker are his closest living relatives.

The two horse types are both desert equines, resistant to heat and able to survive on meagre rations of feed and water. The Akhal-Teke and Caspian represent types 1 and 2, and the Arab – the founding father of all modern hotblooded breeds – is their most noteworthy descendant.

Zebra

Ancient primitive horses like those described above are known to have had distinctive zebra-like stripes on their legs, which served as camouflage in their natural environment. The zebra herds of Africa are direct descendants of these primitive horses, and the fact that they still exist in the wild proves the efficacy of this camouflaging. Today, there are three distinct types of zebra.

Grevy's zebra

This is the largest zebra, standing about 13.2 hands. He is a striking creature, with a long head, slender physique and narrow striping, which extends down his legs, leaving only his belly white. His black dorsal stripe is offset by bands of white on either side, and his mane is black-tipped and erect.

The Grevy's zebra is the largest and most handsome of the zebra varieties.

Grevy's zebra are mostly confined to northern Kenya, east of the Great Rift Valley, although they tend to range into Ethiopia and Somalia. Unlike wild horses, they do not run as stallions with 'harems', instead establishing territories into which females come to foal and to breed.

A Grevy's mare will carry her foal for 13 months – the longest gestation period of any equine. Foals are left in 'kindergartens', guarded by the territorial male, and forage much more quickly than wild horse foals: a six-week-old Grevy's zebra will graze as often as a five-month-old horse, meaning that the zebras become independent of their dams at a younger age.

Plains zebra

The Plains zebra is the most abundant, found distributed throughout eastern and southern Africa. He is a broadly striped, plump little animal with a distinctive 'bark', quite unlike the horse's neigh or ass's bray. There are two subspecies (thought now to be extinct in the wild), Grant's and Burchell's, the latter having a reddish-yellow colouring and lack of stripes on his hindquarters.

The Quagga, once thought to be a separate species, is now believed to be a derivative of the Plains zebra and is extinct, although efforts have been made to reconstruct it.

Grant's zebra is a sub-species of the Plains type – like the Burchell's, he has a distinctive 'bark' as opposed to the bray of an ass or a horse's neigh.

The Plains zebra – covered in distinctive, broad stripes – is the most abundant and is usually the strain found in zoos and circuses.

The Plains species is the zebra most likely to be seen in captivity, whether in zoos or circuses. He is an easy keeper, but is intelligent and wilful, which is perhaps where he gets his reputation as being difficult to train.

The Plains zebra has reddish-yellow colouring, which makes him easy to determine from the striking Grevy's.

Mountain zebra

There are also two subspecies of the third type, the Mountain zebra. Hartmann's occupies the rugged terrain at the edge of the African plateau east of the Namib Desert. In the mid-20th century there were as many as 75,000 Mountain zebra, which were regarded as vermin by African livestock farmers, whose cattle competed with the striped equines for forage and water. Stampeding zebra caused a great deal of damage, and by 1973 Hartmann's was considered endangered, with only about 7,000 remaining. Hartmann's zebra produces a neigh similar to that of the horse.

The Cape Mountain zebra is the smallest, standing less than 12 hands. He is stockier than Hartmann's, with broad black stripes closely spaced over a white body. He formerly inhabited the mountain ranges of the southern Cape Province and almost died out, with only about 140 remaining in the 1960s. Today, he is protected and nurtured in the Mountain Zebra National Park and Cape Point Nature Reserve.

The Cape Mountain zebra is the smallest of all types, standing less than 12 hands, and is today a protected species.

Gaits

All equines have four main gaits – walk, trot, canter and gallop – but there are also 'five-gaited' breeds, the majority of which come from the Americas. It has been suggested that most horses were originally pacers, but the introduction of carts and carriages meant that the trot became more desirable and pacers were increasingly bred out. It is said that fifth gaits cannot be taught: the horse possesses them naturally.

Four basic gaits

Walk One-two-three-four beat gait, with the horse moving freely and athletically.
Trot Two-beat diagonal gait, in which the rider traditionally 'posts' or rises on every other beat.
Canter Comfortable semi-fast, three-beat gait.
Gallop The fastest gait – racehorses can gallop at speeds of up to 72 kmph (45 mph) – in which all four feet leave the ground at once.

Fifth gaits

Pace Smooth, lateral gait, the sequence being right hind, right fore, left hind, left fore, the hind foot touching the ground a fraction of a second before the front foot. When performed on a hard surface, a definite one-two-three-four beat can be heard.
Running walk Between the pace and the trot, this is properly an 'even' gait, neither diagonal nor lateral. It is a four-beat gait, independent in the set-down and pick-up of the hooves. The hoof support sequence is two hooves flat on the ground and then three hooves on the ground.
Fox trot Found in the Missouri Fox Trotter, this is a diagonal gait, in which the horse appears to walk with his forelegs while running with his hindlegs.
Rack or single-foot Fast, even gait in which each foot meets the ground separately at equal intervals, with only one foot striking the ground at a time.
Tölt Found in the Icelandic Horse, the *tölt* is a lateral, four-beat running walk at which the horse can move with explosive speed.
More detail on these gaits is provided in the individual breed profiles.

Arab

conformation elegant head with noticeably dished profile, curved neck, sloping shoulders, short back, hard, clean limbs
colour all solid colours, except palomino
height 14.2–15 hands
uses riding, showing, endurance, racing

He is the son of the desert, the drinker of the wind, and to the Arabian people he is *keheilan* – literally, pure blood. For thousands of years, the hotblooded Arab has been sought after as the most pure and most ancient of all the world's horses. He is the epitome of equine beauty, from the bright blaze of his fine eyes to the very tip of his flamboyant tail.

The Arab is the fountainhead of modern breeding, his descendants forming the foundation of the Thoroughbred, which is coveted worldwide for his speed.

There are records of the Arabian breed going back as far as 3,000 BC, although it cannot now be gauged how much of this is fact. Arab horses were kept by the Bedouin people, by whom they were highly prized for their beauty and fire, their turn of foot and hardiness. They were able to thrive on meagre rations and their fleetness was essential for lightning raids on rival tribes.

When the Prophet Mohammed declared that 'no evil spirit will dare enter a tent where there is a purebred horse', and asserted that those treating the horse with respect would be rewarded in the afterlife, the Arab became even further revered. The Bedouin tribes strove to keep the breed *asil* (pure), and use of any foreign blood was strictly forbidden.

The Arabian horse became not simply a conveyance of war, but a status symbol. Tribal leaders preferred to use mares in forays to enemy camps, because they were less likely to whicker to other horses and thus warn the enemy of their impending arrival.

Mare families were named for the sheikh who bred them, and five distinct families evolved: Kehilan, Seglawi, Abeyan, Hamdani and Habdan. These five strains were easily identifiable and formed the basis for the modern Arab.

He is unique among the horse breeds in that he has 17 ribs, 5 lumbar vertebrae and 16 tail bones – all other breeds have 18 ribs, 6 lumbar vertebrae and 18 tail bones. His beautiful head shows the *jibbah* – a distinctive shield-shaped bulge between the eyes found in no other horse breed. His other unique feature is the *mitbah*, the angle where the head meets the neck, resulting in a fine arching curve that enables his head to be extremely flexible and mobile. He has small, curved ears and large, expressive eyes.

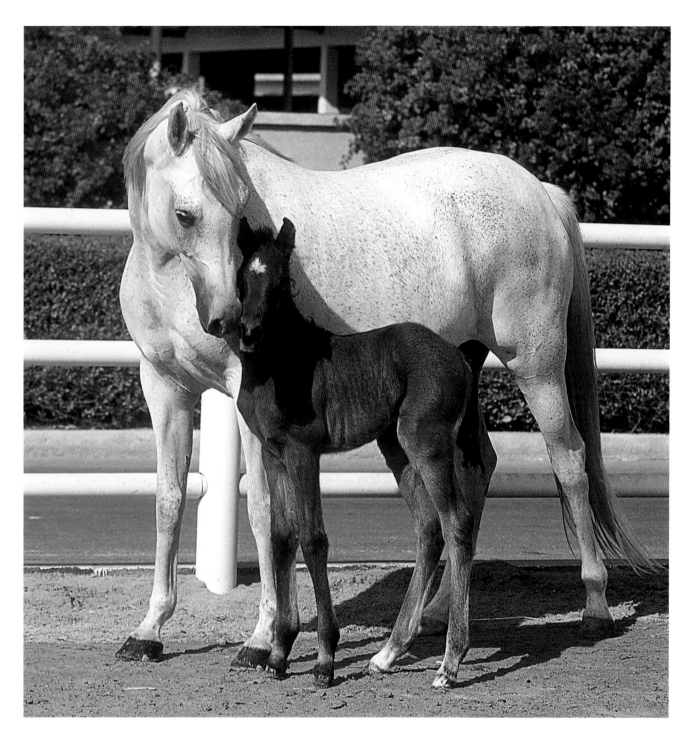

Other than palomino, all solid colours are permitted in the modern Arab – including black, which the desert breeders endeavoured to eliminate because it absorbed heat. The speed and stamina so prized by the Bedouin people remain his abiding characteristics and today the Arab excels in racing and endurance riding.

'no evil spirit will dare enter a tent where there is a purebred horse'

Shagya Arab

conformation fine head, elegant neck, sloping shoulder, good limbs and feet
colour predominantly grey, also bay, chestnut, black
height 15–16 hands
uses competition, harness, all-rounder

If the purebred Arab is the equine 'diamond', the Shagya could be said to be the 'brilliant' – cut and polished to perfection. This rare breed was developed two centuries ago to fulfil demand for the ultimate riding and harness horse, and combines the beauty and endurance of the purebred with the height and strength of the modern riding horse.

The new breed was started in 1789 at the Babolna Stud, Hungary, but takes its name from a dapple grey stallion foaled in 1830. Shagya was bred by the Bani Saher bedouin tribe in what was then Syria and came to Babolna in 1836. Highly prepotent and immensely fertile, he appears in almost all Shagya pedigrees, giving the breed both his type and his name.

While the stallion lines of the Shagya breed were almost all desert-bred Arabians, and the mares used also showed Arab influence, English Thoroughbred and Lipizzaner blood was introduced to add height and substance.

Since the breed's beginnings, meticulous records have been kept detailing not only the lineage, colour and measurements of all the stallions and mares used, but also other characteristics of individuals and their offspring. Among all the world's horses, only the purebred Arabian can boast such long and complete pedigrees.

Thoroughbred

conformation refined head, long neck, high withers (highest
    part of the back), well-muscled shoulders, clean legs
colour bay, chestnut, brown, black, grey
height 16 hands
uses racing, performance horse

Whether on the Kentucky dirt, among the opulence of Dubai or in the quintessential Englishness of Royal Ascot, the Thoroughbred is revered the world over for both his fire and his might. This equine powerhouse can sprint up to 72 kmph (45 mph) and, at speed, can jump a length of 10 m (30 ft).

It is no coincidence that racing is called the Sport of Kings. It is widely believed that King Richard I (Richard the Lionheart) devised the first horserace – on Epsom Downs in England, now home to the world-famous Derby. King James I set up the first racecourse at Newmarket, a town universally known as the headquarters of modern English horseracing.

But the native running horses – probably a mixture of Spanish, Barb, Irish Hobby and Scottish Galloway – although strong, were not fast enough, and needed the refinement of Arab blood. The word Thoroughbred comes from the Arabian *keheilan* (pure blood). Some 93 per cent of all Thoroughbreds can be traced back to just three sires: the Byerley Turk, the Darley Arabian and the Godolphin Arabian, named for the men who owned them.

The Byerley Turk – despite his name, he was probably an Arab or an Akhal-Teke – was captured by Captain Robert Byerley at the siege of Buda. One of his direct descendants was Herod, who himself became a distinguished sire in both Europe and America. From Herod's line came Diomed, winner of the first Epsom Derby in 1780 and sire of some of the most famous horses in American racing history.

The Darley Arabian was bought in Syria by Thomas Darley in 1704. He was the great-great-grandfather of Eclipse, perhaps the most famous racehorse of all time, who was unbeaten in his 18 races. The Darley Arabian also sired Bulle Rock, the first Thoroughbred to reach American shores when he was exported to Virginia in 1730.

It was once said that 'the blood of the Godolphin Arabian is in every stable in England', although he was originally used as a 'teaser' to test mares for other stallions. But at stud, he fought another stallion for the mare Roxana, from whom he sired Cade. Cade was the father of Matchem, whose offspring were to prove particularly influential in the history of American racehorses.

Legend has it that the Godolphin Arabian was discovered pulling a cart in France and brought to England by his purchaser, Edward Coke, who in turn sold him to the Earl of Godolphin. The 'Coke Arabian' would not have had quite the same ring to it.

'This equine powerhouse can sprint at up to 72 kmph (45 mph) and can jump a length of 10 m (30 ft).'

Barb

conformation long head with straight or convex profile, upright shoulders, short, strong back, deep girth, small, narrow feet
colour chestnut, bay, grey, black
height 14.2–15.2 hands
uses riding, crossbreeding

Like his better known neighbour, the Arab, the Barb has had a profound influence on the world's horse breeds. Indeed, some believe that the Godolphin Arabian – one of the Thoroughbred's three foundation sires – was actually a Barb.

The Barb is native to North Africa and, like the Arab, is a desert horse – but there the similarity ends. He stands slightly taller, with a straight or even convex profile, which can also be seen in the Andalucian and Lusitano, in whose development the Barb played a major role. His influence is also evident in the white horses of the Camargue, and in the breeds of North and South America, notably the Mustang.

The original Barb was a warhorse, highly prized for his agility and turn of foot – he is lightning fast over short distances – although less so for his uncertain temper. He was used by the Ishmaelites and the Berbers, and it was from the latter, who were notoriously barbaric, that he took his name.

These marauding tribes swept across Africa, Spain, Portugal and parts of France, and by the time they were finally vanquished their strong and swift horses were established as valuable breeding stock.

Alter-Real

conformation small head, strong shoulders, short body, deep girth, hard legs
colour bay, brown, grey, occasionally chestnut
height 15–16 hands
uses quality riding horse, suitable for High School

If the Iberian kings – the magnificent Andalucian and the noble Lusitano – can be said to have a poor relation, it is perhaps Portugal's Alter-Real, even though the 'Real' part of his name means 'royal'.

The breed was established in 1748 in Alentejo to provide horses for the Royal Stables at Lisbon. These horses had to be suitable for classical equitation and carriage driving. After eight years the stud was moved to Altér, a town known for its mineral-rich soil and nutritious grazing, from which the breed received the first part of its name.

The Alter-Real's foundation was 300 fine Andalucian mares imported from Jerez, Spain, and Arabian stallions. The stud was sacked by Napoleon's troops, who took the best stock for the Peninsular War (1804–14). Attempts were made thereafter to upgrade remaining stock using Hanoverian, Arabian and English bloodlines, but it was not until the further introduction of Andalucian blood in the late 19th century that the fortunes of the Alter-Real improved.

Portugal's equine expert Dr Ruy D'Andrade saved a small percentage of breeding stock from which he line-bred two stallions. In 1932 the stud was given to the Portuguese Ministry of Agriculture, which has further improved it by culling unsuitable mares and using only the finest sires.

Andalucian

conformation noble head with pronounced convex nose,
small ears, crested neck, powerful shoulders,
short-coupled
colour predominantly grey, also black, bay, roan
height 15–16 hands
uses all-round riding, suitable for High School

In London's Trafalgar Square there stands a statue of King Charles I mounted on a powerful horse. It is no coincidence that his magnificent steed bears a striking resemblance to the Andalucian – King Philippe II of Spain unified the breed and used only those horses closest to the stylized ideal of paintings and sculptures.

But the Andalucian, who takes his name from the sun-soaked southern region of Spain, is among the most ancient of the world's breeds – cave drawings have been found near Malaga dating back as far as 20,000 BC, that clearly depict horses very similar to today's native equine.

The Andalucian is thought to be related to the Barb, and has had almost as much influence on the development of the horse as the Arabian. His ancestors were taken to the New World by the conquistadors in the 16th century and his influence can be seen in the Criollo, Paso Fino, Mustang and Appaloosa, among others.

Swift and agile, biddable and brave, he was the warhorse of kings, until the need for heavier horses to carry the weighty armoury of the Middle Ages. But with the introduction of firearms in the 15th century, the Andalucian, with his intelligence and spirit, again became the cavalry's choice.

Later, his high-stepping gait, proud bearing and flamboyant beauty put him centre stage as the epitome of the High School – or *haute école* – of classical riding. Today's renowned 'dancing white horse', the Lipizzaner, is closely related to the Andalucian – hence the Spanish Riding School of Vienna. His bravery and agility also made him ideally suited to the bullring.

The Andalucian fell out of favour again in the 19th century, and it was only thanks to the Monastry of Cartuja, which continued to breed Spain's national equine, that he did not disappear completely. The Carthusian monks kept a small stud from which they bred only the finest examples to preserve the beauty of the *caballo pura raza Espanola* – the purebred Spanish horse.

And beautiful he undoubtedly is. Some 80 per cent of modern Andalucians are grey, although other solid colours are permitted. The horse retains the proud bearing of his ancient ancestors, and his fine head shows the classic Roman profile, balanced by a broad forehead, expressive eyes and inverted 'comma' nostrils. His crested neck and muscular shoulders, compact body and sloping croup give him power as well as grace, and this mighty breed is still coveted today as life imitating art.

Lusitano

conformation convex, hawk-like profile, powerful arched neck, upright shoulders, compact body, fine, clean legs
colour all solid colours
height 15.1–16 hands
uses dressage, riding, harness

We are all familiar with the legend of the centaur, the hybrid half-man/half-horse of fable, but it is thought that the skill of the Iberian horsemen and their eerie unity with their muscular mounts gave rise to the myth. Legend also has it that the Lusitano mares were sired by the wind, Zephyr, whose speed they passed on to their progeny.

The Iberian horsemen invaded the European peninsular and gave it its name – and their horses, mixed with indigenous stock, were the cornerstones for the purebred Spanish horse. These horses are mentioned by Homer in his celebrated work of 1100 BC, *The Iliad*, and by the renowned cavalryman Xenophon, who is widely credited with developing the art of modern horsemanship.

Xenophon was full of praise for the Iberian horses and horsemen, and around 370 BC enthused about their war techniques, which consisted of charges by a single mounted warrior with pirouettes and sudden stops and starts, repeated many times. Was this perhaps the basis of the 'airs above the ground' of the Spanish Riding School of Vienna, and the very foundation of modern dressage?

The Portuguese Lusitano bears a strong resemblance to his Spanish cousin, the Andalucian, and his ancestors were likely Sorraias – the occasional dun colouring seen in the Lusitano is probably a throwback to those horses. An interesting theory is that Sorraia stock migrated across the Gibraltar peninsula into North Africa in prehistoric times – meaning that, rather than the Barb horse being the forefather of the Iberian, the exact opposite may be true. Whichever way round it was, the exchange of equine influence was undoubtedly beneficial to both horses. The Barb of today certainly resembles Iberian horses.

The Lusitano stands a little taller and has a more convex profile than the Andalucian, which has been refined with Arabian blood. He does, however, have the same noble bearing, turn of foot and natural athleticism, which undoubtedly served him well as a warhorse in the Middle Ages, while his agility makes him now an exceptional performance horse. It also makes him invaluable in the bullrings of modern Portugal – he is named after the old name for the region, Lusitania.

Bullfighting in Portugal differs from that in Spain, in that the object of the fight is not so much to dispatch the bull but to demonstrate the training and the schooling of the horse, and it is considered a great dishonour to the *rejoneador* – bullfighter – if his horse is injured during the contest. These modern-day cavaliers value their glorious equines – and who can blame them?

Sorraia

conformation convex head, black-tipped ears, strong neck, sloping croup, low-set tail
colour dun, particularly grulla/grullo (grey dun) with black mane and tail
height 13.2–14 hands
uses harness, riding

When you compare him to the powerful Andalucian and the elegant Lusitano, it is difficult to believe that the unassuming little Sorraia is their ancestor. This indigenous Iberian equine – his conformation makes him a horse, rather than a pony – takes his name from the areas around the rivers Sor and Raia, which run through Portugal and Spain, where he was discovered in 1920 by Dr Ruy D'Andrade. He is also known as *marismeno*, the 'horse of the swamp'.

The Sorraia is thought to be a descendant of Przewalski's Horse and the Tarpan. He is nothing special to look at, but his agility made him a superb stockman's horse, used to herd the wild bulls of southern Iberia.

The Sorraia is always dun or grulla/grullo in colour, with black points and zebra stripes on the legs – foals are born with a zebra-like pattern all over. These colorations provided him with excellent camouflage in his native environment.

It is believed the Sorraia was taken to the Americas with the conquistadors, and very similar DNA has been found in America's wild horse, the Mustang, among which the Sorraia's distinctive grey-dun colouring still appears.

Today, this little horse is on the edge of extinction. It was only through the dedication of Dr D'Andrade – who selected 30 of these horses to run as a protected herd – that the Sorraia did not die out altogether.

Dartmoor

conformation small, pretty head, medium-length neck, sloping shoulders, long back

colour brown, bay, black, chestnut, occasionally roan, grey, few or no white markings

height 12.2 hands

uses riding, harness, pack pony

There are references to the Dartmoor pony, indigenous to the moorland in Devon for which he is named, as far back as the 11th century, but little is known about the origins of this stocky little breed. Ponies have been running on the moor for millennia, and have changed very little. He has a kind disposition and is easily trainable.

Thrifty and strong, the Dartmoor made a superb pack pony and was invaluable for working on the farms around the moor. At the beginning of the 20th century, when people began to register their ponies, the bigger animal, standing up to 14 hands, was most popular. But left to their own devices on the moor, the smaller pony held the natural advantage, being able to withstand the harsh weather with little shelter. In turn, the pony has helped to conserve the moor itself, keeping tree numbers under control.

Sadly, the Dartmoor pony is now listed by the Rare Breeds Survival Trust as 'vulnerable', with fewer than 500 breeding females left, although the Moorland Scheme launched in 1998 to preserve the true Dartmoor type in its natural environment has slowly increased numbers.

Exmoor

conformation small, neat head with small ears, deep chest, broad and level back, short legs with good, hard feet
colour bay, brown, dun with distinctive mealy markings around muzzle, no white markings
height 12.2–13 hands
uses riding, driving, showing, long-distance

Independent and intelligent, the Exmoor pony is supremely adapted to his native moorland environment and retains several unique features designed to protect him from the elements. These include the 'toad' eye, which has a fleshy hood above and below to keep out wind and rain; a double-layered waterproof winter coat – effectively, a short, fine layer of 'thermal underwear' and a hard, greasy raincoat – and a 'snow chute' on the tail consisting of a fan of short hairs by the root that funnels off rainwater. His large, strong teeth enable him to chew tough vegetation and his well-sprung ribs give his digestive system plenty of room to process it.

Unlike many of Britain's other mountain and moorland equines, the ponies on Exmoor have remained remarkably unchanged – ancient horse bones found in caves in the nearby Mendip Hills are identical to those of modern Exmoor ponies. A Spanish stallion named Katerfelto ran with the local herds around 1815, although it has never been established how he got there. He was dun with a black dorsal stripe, and dun Exmoor ponies are still seen today – the only other colour besides bay and brown permitted. But no other equine blood has been introduced to 'improve' the ponies.

Until the early 19th century, Exmoor itself – which spans the borders of Somerset and Devon in southwest England – was a designated 'royal forest', a hunting ground owned by the Crown and managed by a warden to whom local farmers paid a sum for grazing rights. Then the moor was sold to an industrialist called John Knight and the warden, Thomas Acland, took a band of 30 Exmoor ponies from which to continue to breed the true Exmoor type. The Acland ponies thrived and formed the basis of the famous Anchor herd, which still exists on the moor today.

The closest the Exmoor pony came to being wiped out completely was during World War II, when troops were trained on the moor and used its wildlife, including the native ponies, for target practice. By the end of the war, only about 50 Exmoor ponies remained. The breed has enjoyed a change of fortunes since then, although it is still listed as 'endangered' by the Rare Breeds Survival Trust. There are fewer than 200 still free-living on the moor and fewer than 1,200 breeding animals in total.

The little Exmoor has great charm, and his sweet nature and tough constitution make him an ideal family pony, kind enough to carry children and strong enough to be ridden by adults or broken to harness.

'ancient horse bones
found in caves in the
nearby Mendip Hills
are identical to those of
modern Exmoor ponies.'

Connemara

conformation pony head of medium length, good length of
    rein, sloping shoulders, compact, well-balanced body
colour predominantly grey, though all solid colours
    permitted, including palomino and dark-eyed cream
height 12.2–14.2 hands
uses riding, endurance, jumping, hunting

Like the lunar landscape of the region from which he takes his name, Ireland's Connemara pony is tough and rugged, suited to the harsh terrain and inclement climate.

Said to be Ireland's only indigenous breed, the Connemara dates back some 2,500 years, when Celtic warriors brought their dun ponies to the island and used them to draw chariots and carts. Legend also has it that horses from the Spanish Armada, wrecked off the treacherous coast of Ireland in 1588, swam to shore and mated with local stock. There may be aspects of truth in both versions. Either way, the Connemara is a hardy mountain and moorland pony, able to thrive on sparse rations and surefooted enough to survive on the rocky coastline, where one wrong step could send him crashing to a certain death.

Farmers in the area later caught and tamed these wild ponies, which could pull a cart with a heavy load with ease and helped to share the burden with the poor farmers, who usually had large families for whom to provide. They could only afford to keep one pony and it would usually be a mare, from which they could breed a foal to sell to augment their income when times were hard.

The carts were used to transport rocks to clear the land, to bring loads of seaweed from the shore to serve as fertilizer, and to carry turf cut from the bogs, which was used as fuel for cooking and heat. On Sundays, the day of rest, the cart would carry the farmer and his family to Mass. No rest for the Connemara pony. Consequently, these mares were strong and agile, of generally kind disposition and from proven breeding stock – all good qualities from which to breed a viable native pony.

It was not until the beginning of the 20th century, when more ponies were kept in stables and hence the breed lost some of its hardiness, that the Connemara Pony Society was formed to both preserve and refine the breed. A further concern was that random crossing with other bloodlines was also having a detrimental effect on the breed, although the introduction of Arabian and Thoroughbred blood had improved the native stock in the 1700s. A carefully selected band of about a dozen ponies was turned out into the wild to ensure the Connemara continued to thrive in the way it had centuries before. The Society acheived its aim. Those ponies that survived had excellent qualities and preserved the purity of the pony. Today's Connemara is a compact, well-built pony with a handsome head and kind eye. He is a quality riding type with scope, intelligence and stamina.

'a pony as tough and rugged as the lunar landscape of the region from which he takes his name'

Fell

conformation small chiselled head, sloping shoulders,
   well-muscled hindquarters, low-set hocks
colour predominantly black, also bay, brown, grey,
   no white markings
height 13–14 hands
uses riding, harness, packhorse, all-rounder

The Fell has been recognized since Roman times and is thought to have evolved from local northern English ponies being mated with French, Friesian, German, Polish or Spanish horses brought by back-up troops manning Hadrian's Wall, the Roman boundary between England and Scotland. The result was a sturdy, strong pony that could carry a full-grown man with ease.

He was a superlative packhorse, strong, surefooted and placid, and a surviving network of 'packways' that winds through much of northern England traces his hoofprints across the region as he pulled loads of wool, slate, copper and lead. The advent of the railways in the middle of the 19th century made the pony redundant as a means of transport and many were sold abroad for slaughter, but the Fell survived in his native Cumbria and is now used as a riding animal for both children and adults.

A combination of his fast walk and smooth paces make the Fell a comfortable ride, and his agility means he is a superb hunter. Highly trainable, he is also suited to the increasingly popular sport of driving. Queen Elizabeth II breeds Fell ponies, which are competed in four-in-hand carriage driving by her husband, the Duke of Edinburgh.

Dales

conformation neat head, deep shoulders, short back, strong loins, hard feet
colour predominantly black, also bay, brown, grey, occasional roan, no white markings
height 14.2 hands
uses riding, harness, packhorse, all-rounder

On the other side of northern England, the Dales pony, like the Fell – which he closely resembles – was used as a pack animal, his strength and speed a bonus to the merchants who transported lead across the Pennine Hills. Nimble and hardy, he could cross the rugged terrain with ease, sometimes travelling up to 400 km (250 miles) in a week.

The same strength and agility made the Dales invaluable to the hill farmers and shepherds, and he also shone in the popular trotting races of the era. Norfolk and Yorkshire Trotters were bred to Dales mares, resulting in the swift, flashy trot the breed still exhibits today. In times of war, the ponies were used by the artillery as packhorses, and many were conscripted. There is a story of one farmer who, while his beloved Dales pony stood hidden in his kitchen, entertained an army captain in his sitting room.

The Dales stands slightly taller than the Fell and also bears a slight resemblance to the Welsh Cob – indeed, a Welsh stallion called Comet was used extensively on Dales mares in the 19th century to add bone and substance to the modern breed.

Highland

conformation fine, tapered head, powerful neck,
    well-proportioned body, high-set tail, good legs
colour all shades of dun, grey, black, bay, but all
    solid colours permitted
height 13–14.2 hands
uses all-rounder

It is said that the Highland breed is 'too old to know how old it is', and certainly there have been native ponies in the Highland region and Western Isles of Scotland since at least 8 BC. Whether they came with the retreat of the last glaciers 10,000 years ago or were brought by prehistoric settlers is open to debate, but today's ponies still exhibit the 'primitive' markings of the earliest equine ancestors – the only British native breed that continues to do so with no conscious breeding selection.

There are two distinct types of Highland pony – the larger, heavier mainland type and his smaller, finer Western Isles cousin. Both are supremely adapted to the unforgiving Scottish climate, with a winter coat of strong badger-like hair over a soft, dense undercoat. All colours are permitted, and the primitive dun colour in all its varieties – mouse, silver, yellow, grey and cream – still occurs, with many ponies also having zebra markings on their legs and a dorsal stripe. These colours can be seen in the feral ponies on the Isle of Rum.

The Highland is strong and agile, and makes an excellent family all-rounder. The ponies have the scope to be good jumpers and are trainable enough to hold their own in the dressage arena.

Shetland

conformation neat head, thick neck, powerful
    shoulders, well-formed hindquarters, broad loins,
    thick mane and tail
colour all colours, including piebald and skewbald
height 86–107 cm (34–42 in)
uses riding, harness

Despite his small stature, the Shetland – said to be the oldest British native breed – can carry a full-grown man. There is some debate as to whether the ponies were brought to the Shetland Isles by the Vikings, but small ponies are certainly depicted on the Papal and Bressay Stones found on Shetland dating from the 9th century – one shows a monk astride a tiny, elegantly proportioned equine.

The Shetland ponies were highly revered by the islanders, each depending on the other for survival. Strong and hardy, the ponies were good doers and could carry heavy loads with ease, while their coarse mane and tail hair provided the raw materials for fishing nets and lines, and excellent stuffing for mattresses.

When a law was passed in the 19th century forbidding children to work in the coal mines, the Shetland's strength and size made him a perfect substitute, with ponies being bred specifically for use underground.

Today, the gentle Shetland is still very popular as a riding pony for both children and adults, although demand for ever-smaller ponies has meant an increase in 'miniatures' – less than 86 cm (34 in) tall – and fewer of the traditional or 'standard' ponies.

New Forest

conformation attractive though horse-like head, longish
    neck, narrow back, good hindquarters, high-set tail
colour all solid colours except blue-eyed cream
height 12.2–14 hands
uses riding

There are records of ponies in the New Forest on England's south coast in 1016, and during the Middle Ages a royal stud was maintained there. Commoners owned grazing rights on the Forest for their ponies, and these still exist today. Every year the ponies are rounded up in the annual 'drift' and either kept on the Forest for breeding or sold at auction.

The idea was that the best stock was retained for breeding, but sadly, this was not always the case. The commoners sold the best ponies for the highest possible price, with the remaining 'worthless' ones left to run on the Forest and breed unchecked. However, over the years Welsh, Dartmoor, Exmoor, Highland, Dales and Arab blood has been introduced to improve the breed and add size and substance. A polo pony called Field Marshall, who stood at stud in the Forest in 1918–19, had considerable influence.

The modern New Forest is agile, intelligent and tough, his narrower build than most native breeds making him an ideal child's pony. His sloping shoulder means he gives a comfortable ride, and he is strong enough to carry an adult.

Welsh Mountain Pony (section A)

conformation small, concave head, sloping
  shoulders, deep girth, slender legs, good feet
colour all solid colours
height 12 hands
uses child's pony, harness

There is no mistaking the Arab influence in the Welsh Mountain Pony, the original and smallest of the four Welsh breeds (section A in the Welsh studbook). Wild ponies are known to have roamed the Welsh mountains since Roman times – Julius Caesar established a stud at Lake Bala in Merionethshire – and they are thought to have descended from the Celtic pony. The climate was harsh and the terrain perilous, so only the hardiest and most surefooted survived, qualities that remain in the breed today.

The Romans introduced Arabian blood to improve and refine existing stock, and this infusion can be seen in the pony's neat, dished face, tiny, curved ears and bold eyes. It is possible, too, that some Thoroughbred and Hackney blood was used. However, the Welsh Mountain Pony has retained his unique characteristics, and makes a superb outcross to other breeds. He is far from being just a pretty toy. Spirited and brave, strong and intelligent, he also possesses an innate gentleness that makes him an ideal child's pony. In addition, he has a good jump and goes well in harness.

The Welsh Mountain Pony was used as the foundation stock for the other three Welsh breeds (see overleaf).

Welsh Pony (section B)

conformation elegant pony head, long, curved neck,
  fine withers, well-balanced body, slender legs
colour all solid colours
height 13–13.2 hands
uses riding pony, harness

As popular as the Welsh Mountain Pony was, there was still demand for a slightly larger, finer type of riding pony, and hence the Welsh Pony (section B) was developed. Bred by using a stallion called Merlin – a direct descendant of the Darley Arabian (see page 18) – on section A mares, the Welsh Pony was sometimes called Merlin's. It is also believed that Welsh Pony of Cob Type (section C) was introduced.

The Welsh Pony retains all the characteristics and sweet temper of his smaller counterpart but is a more quality animal, with natural jumping ability and a lower, smoother action. Surefooted and fast, he was a boon to the Welsh hill farmers, who relied on him as their primary form of transport, but today his fine head and well-balanced body are much admired in the showring and he can turn his hoof to almost any sport, which makes him ideal for a keen young rider.

Like his smaller cousin the Welsh Mountain Pony, the section B is renowned for his quality and substance as well as his versatility and kindness, and as a result Welsh Ponies have been exported all over the world, with Canada, America and Australia forming their own breed societies.

Welsh Pony of Cob Type (section C)

conformation pony head, sloping shoulders, compact, deep body, strong loins, short, muscular legs
colour all solid colours
height 13.2 hands
uses riding, harness

Infusions of blood from the Andalucian, the now extinct Pembroke Carthorse, the Norfolk Trotter and – more latterly – the Hackney have produced in the Welsh Pony of Cob Type (section C) a versatile all-rounder that retains pony characteristics and the best qualities of the Welsh Mountain.

It is believed that the Romans crossed their own horses with Welsh Mountain Ponies before the Spanish blood was introduced, but the latter is well documented: in the 12th century, the Archdeacon of Brecon, Giraldus Cambrensis (Gerald of Wales), wrote 'There are in mid-Wales most excellent studs, deriving their origins from some fine Spanish horses.'

The pony was formerly known as the Powys Horse and was further refined with Arab and Thoroughbred blood. Later, four stallions in particular had great influence – Trotting Comet (1840), True Briton (1830), Cymro Llwyd (1850) and Alonzo the Brave (1860). The modern section C is bigger than both sections A and B, standing around 13.2 hands, which means he can carry an adult with ease. Active and hardy, he excels in harness as well as under saddle, and is renowned for his equable temperament and inherent common sense.

Welsh Cob (section D)

conformation elegant dished head, arched neck, short-coupled, strong back and loins, well-shaped feet
colour all solid colours
height 14.2 and over – there is no upper height limit
uses riding, harness, all-rounder

In silhouette, the Welsh Cob (section D of the studbook) looks like a scaled-up version of the Welsh Mountain Pony. He is elegant, strong and courageous, renowned for his endurance and high-stepping extravagant trot. This last is perhaps the result of Norfolk Trotters and Yorkshire Coach Horses, whose blood was introduced to Welsh stock in the 18th and 19th centuries to add height and substance.

Trotting Comet, whose influence made an impact on both sections C and D, was a trotting horse, while True Briton was by a Yorkshire Coach Horse out of an Arab mare. Cymro Llwyd was by the Crawshay Bailey Arab out of a trotting mare, and his palomino colouring is still seen in Welsh Cobs today. Alonzo the Brave stood 16 hands and was of Hackney stock, although he can be traced back to the Darley Arabian (see page 18).

The Welsh Cob has served many masters – his stamina and robust good nature made him the army's choice, both for hauling heavy equipment and for the mounted regiments; he has also been cosseted by royalty and has worked on the lowly farms of the poor. Crossed with a Thoroughbred, today's Welsh Cob produces a superior competition horse.

Hackney

conformation slightly convex profile, arched neck, strong, low shoulders, low-set hocks, high-set tail
colour bay, brown, chestnut, black
height 15 hands
uses predominantly harness, also a comfortable ride

Before the advent of the car, horses provided the only form of transport. Farmers relied on them to work the land, take them to market, the family to church and provide the occasional day's hunting. The word Hackney derives from the French *haquenée* (a language commonly spoken in England in medieval times), which describes an all-purpose horse with stamina, pace and soundness.

The Hackney's extravagant high-stepping action evolved relatively recently. In the 18th century, Arab blood was introduced to the native Hackney horses to refine the breed without drastically changing it – indeed, the Hackney tends to be influential in breeding, rather than influenced. As carriages became more sophisticated and tastes increasingly flamboyant, demand increased for a showy horse with a flashy trot and the Hackney became a status symbol.

As the car grew in popularity, he became more of a show horse and the modern Hackney is spectacular – elegant and athletic, with great stamina and presence.

Fell and Welsh blood was used in the late 19th century to produce a Hackney pony – not just a miniature version of the horse, but a show animal with real pony quality.

'The word Hackney derives from the French haquenée *for an all-purpose horse.'*

Cleveland Bay

conformation 'hawk-like' head, well-muscled neck,
    well-ribbed body, clean legs, hard feet
colour bay, little or no white markings
height 16–16.2 hands
uses harness, dressage, showjumping

The Cleveland Bay is Britain's oldest indigenous horse breed, dating back to the 17th century when oriental – probably Barb – blood used on native bay mares produced a strong, durable breed of uniform size, colour and substance.

Originally known as the Chapman horse, after the packmen who used him, he was later named the Cleveland Bay after the region from which he came. A superlative coach horse, in the late 18th century Thoroughbred blood was introduced to produce a bigger, faster animal known as the Yorkshire Coach Horse, which became popular worldwide during the golden age of coaching.

With the arrival of the car, the Cleveland Bay fell from favour and numbers declined further during World War I, when he was used as an artillery horse. The determination of the Yorkshire breeders kept the Cleveland Bay going, but by 1960 there were only five or six stallions remaining. The breed has since enjoyed a revival – they make superb competition horses, whether purebred or crossed with Thoroughbred – but is still listed by the Rare Breeds Survival Trust as 'critical'.

Bold, honest and intelligent, the Cleveland Bay possesses both style and speed, as well as hardiness and longevity. The breed is used by Queen Elizabeth II in ceremonial duties and she is patron of the breed society.

Anglo-Arab

conformation straight, attractive head, long, sloping neck to fine shoulders, long, slender legs, neat feet
colour all solid colours
height 15.3–16.2 hands
uses riding, competition

As his name suggests, the Anglo-Arab is a cross of the Thoroughbred with the Arab. The breed originated in Germany in 1892 at a stud farm in Zweibrücken, and it was the French who perpetuated it.

The aim was to create a horse that combined the strength and speed of the Thoroughbred with the endurance and durability of the Arab. The French equine expert Gayot recommended the process of breeding the progeny of a Thoroughbred/Arab back to a Thoroughbred, then the resulting offspring back to the Arab. After much experimenting, the favoured mix was produced from Pompadour, France, and the Anglo-Arab breed established, although there were still variations.

In broad terms, the Anglo-Arab should have no more than 75 per cent Arab blood, and no less than 25 per cent. He is taller than his oriental forebear and is strong, fast and athletic. He has a bigger build than the Thoroughbred and, while he may not match him for speed, has a far greater jumping ability. He therefore makes a good competition horse; trainable, tough and good-looking, he excels at dressage, showing and showjumping.

Ariègeois

conformation small, fine head, thick mane, long back,
    tendency towards cowhocks, good, hard feet
colour black, rust-brown highlights in winter
height 13.1–14.3 hands
uses pack pony, harness, riding

This ancient breed is named for the Ariège River in the Pyrenees Mountains that divide France and Spain, and bears a startling similarity to prehistoric cave drawings found in the region. Perhaps because of the remoteness of the area, there he stayed, without attracting much attention, for thousands of years and it was only in the early 20th century that breeders started to become interested.

Also known as the Merens Pony, this mountain breed is always black with no white markings, although his coat takes on a rusty sheen during the winter months. He strongly resembles England's Fell and Dales ponies and there is certainly some oriental blood, which can be seen in his fine head, perhaps introduced in Roman times.

Surefooted and hardy, the Ariègeois was used as a pack pony and was valued by the smugglers who worked along the Spanish border. He was also to become crucial to hill farmers in the region, for whom the tractor was impractical, and was worked in the mines.

Today, the Ariègeois is still valued as a pack animal, but his calm nature and sweet disposition also make him an ideal child's riding pony.

Furioso

conformation refined head, prominent ears, muscular hindquarters, strong legs, sound feet
colour black, brown
height 16 hands
uses competition horse, harness

This is one of the few breeds named after one stallion, Furioso, born in Hungary in 1836. A Thoroughbred, Furioso was sold to a military stud in Mezöhegyesh, where his breeding career began in 1841. It lasted for ten years, by which time he had left 95 stallions and 81 mares. He proved immensely prepotent – having strong influence on his stock – and hence the lineage was named after him. The breed was valued as a good-quality all-purpose horse.

Part of the breeding operation moved to another two studs in Austria, at Radovec and Piber, but the breed went into decline when Austria and Hungary divided in 1867. To keep it going, another sire, North Star – probably a Thoroughbred, although some accounts say he was a Norfolk Trotter – was introduced in 1870 and the lineages merged, with occasional use of other Thoroughbred blood to refresh things. Breeding continued in both Mezöhegyesh and Radovec, with two distinct types emerging, the former being slightly coarser and bigger. In Radovec, some Nonius blood was introduced to increase endurance and hardiness.

Today the Furioso is comparatively rare, but he is an excellent carriage horse as well as competition mount. His Thoroughbred influence is apparent in his fine profile, sound conformation and straight, true action.

Friesian

conformation noble head, powerful neck,
  compact body, short, strong legs, hard feet
colour black
height 15.3–16.2 hands
uses harness

Powerful and proud, the Friesian is a horse of great beauty and strength. He is thought to date back as far as 1000 BC and comes from the Friesland area, one of 12 provinces of the Netherlands in the northwest of Europe. His development is often credited to monks of the region crossing *Equus robustus* – the huge Forest Horse known to have roamed that part of the continent – with lighter types, producing a heavy but elegant equine with a coat of pure lacquered black.

The people who settled along the coast of the North Sea in 500 BC were farmers, horse breeders, seafarers and tradesman, and their stocky black horse – the only indigenous breed of the Netherlands – was highly prized. Although not a large equine – he is usually around 15 hands, although Friesians standing up to 17 hands have been noted – he is

agile and strong, with an excellent fast trot. This made him desirable as a carriage horse and, in times of war, a cavalry mount. Because of his power, he was able to carry a medieval knight in full armour yet still be able to manoeuvre at speed. This agility was later to make him popular in equitation and in the circus ring.

During the Spanish occupation of the Netherlands in the 80 Years' War (1568–1648), Iberian blood was introduced to the breed, although this is one of the few equines not to have been influenced by the Thoroughbred. The influence of the Andalucian and Lusitano can be seen clearly in his noble head, high knee action and extravagant mane and tail. In turn, the Friesian has been used as foundation stock for other breeds, such as the Oldenburg, the Fell and Dales ponies of England, and the North American Morgan. When the Friesian was almost wiped out after World War I, Oldenburg blood was used to re-establish the breed. The English Black also stemmed from the Friesian and was the basis for the Shire Horse.

The modern Friesian is probably lighter in build than the original breed and is always black with no white markings, although a very small white star on the forehead is permitted. He excels as a carriage horse and is much in demand. His equable temperament and willing character mean that up to ten horses can be driven together – a truly spectacular sight.

'A horse of great beauty and power, in medieval times he was able to carry a knight in full armour.'

Hucul

conformation well-proportioned head, short neck, low withers, compact body, high-set tail
colour predominantly dun, also skewbald and piebald
height 13 hands
uses packhorse, trekking

Whether the Hucul comes from Romania or Poland is open to discussion, due to the countries' borders being moved, but he is known to have originated in the Carpathian Mountains in eastern Europe and is sometimes referred to as the Carpathian Pony.

The Hucul is thought to have existed from around the 13th century, the result of crossbreeding between the Tarpan and Mongolian native ponies – it is the Mongols, one of the nomadic tribes, who are thought to have introduced horses to the region. Because of the climate and conditions, the Hucul was isolated from other equines and so developed into a distinctive breed of great soundness and resistance, as well as being docile and willing. Again, accounts vary as to where the name originated, although part of the Carpathian Mountains region was known as Huzulland.

In 1856, a stud farm for the breed was established in Romania using five foundation sires and the bloodlines were carefully preserved. Today, Huculs are still bred in Romania, as well as Hungary and regions of the former Czechoslovakia and Soviet Union. With more recognition of its better qualities, the breed has become increasingly popular and Huculs are used as pack animals and trekking ponies, the breed's surefootedness being a boon on mountainous routes.

Konik/Tarpan

conformation large head, strong neck, low withers, upright
  shoulders, broad body, deep girth, strong legs
colour dun with black dorsal stripe
height 12–13 hands
uses agriculture, harness

In his native Poland the name Konik means 'small horse', and
although he stands barely 13 hands he has few pony qualities.
He is one of the many pony breeds descended directly from
the prehistoric Tarpan that used to roam the forests of Poland
but was hunted for its meat – which was considered a
delicacy – to extinction. Today the Konik is bred mainly at the
Polish state stud of Jezewice and at Popielno, where careful
selection maintains the breed characteristics.

With his large head, short, strong neck and stocky stature,
the Konik closely resembles the Tarpan, although Arab blood
has been introduced for refinement, and as a result other
colours to the Tarpan's distinctive grey dun, or grulla/grullo,
are sometimes seen. Somewhat ironically, the Konik has been
used – together with Przewalski's Horse (see page 10) – to
recreate the Tarpan, which died out in the late 19th century.
Two German zoologists, Heinz and Lutz Heck, used the two
breeds as well as Icelandic Horses and Swedish Gotlands to
recreate a Tarpan in 1933.

The Polish government has created a preserve for animals
descended from the Tarpan at a forest in Bialowieza and
another in the Popielno Forest. This herd has developed more
and more Tarpan characteristics, and is sometimes referred to
as the Polish Primitive Horse.

Haflinger

conformation pretty head, well-made shoulders, deep girth, long back, excellent legs
colour all shades of chestnut from pale gold to liver, with white or flaxen mane and tail
height 13.2–15 hands
uses riding, harness, forestry

His glorious golden colouring ensures the Haflinger always stands out, but it is not just a case of 'handsome is as handsome does'. He is strong and athletic, with good, smooth paces and a willing, amenable temperament, which make him suitable for almost any equestrian activity – draught work, packing, light harness and combined driving, western and trail riding, endurance riding, dressage and jumping.

The Haflinger takes his name from the village of Hafling, high in the southern Tyrolean Mountains in what are now Austria and Italy, and can be traced back to medieval times. Many of the alpine villages were accessible only by narrow, rocky paths and the surefooted little horse was invaluable to farmers. Artwork from the region from the early 19th century depicts a small but noble horse with packs and riders crossing the steep mountain trails.

The first official documenting of the modern Haflinger appeared in 1874, with the foundation stallion 249 Folie – by the part-bred Arab stallion 133 El' Bedavi XXII out of a native Tyrolean mare. All modern purebred Haflingers must trace back directly to Folie through seven different stallion lines: A, B, M, N, S, ST and W. During World War II, as the military demanded a stronger, sturdier packhorse, the Haflinger breeders produced a shorter, more draught type, but afterwards the emphasis was placed once more on elegance and increased height.

The result was a versatile little horse with a strong constitution, substantial bone and an uncomplicated and people-loving demeanour. And, of course, his unique colour – which ranges from pale gold to rich, vibrant chestnut and covers all shades in between, always with the flamboyant white or flaxen mane and tail. His head is lean and refined, with large, expressive eyes, set well on a medium-length neck with pronounced withers and good, sloping shoulders. He has a deep, broad chest and well-muscled back, and good, strong legs with plenty of bone and hard feet. All in all, a handsome, powerful equine.

The Haflinger's beauty and happy nature make him an ideal family horse, and the breed is now established in five continents, with the first ones arriving in the United States in 1958. In his homeland of Austria, the Haflinger continues to thrive, with a government breeding programme established some 50 years ago.

'The Haflinger's glorious colouring makes him one of the most striking equines.'

Lipizzaner

conformation large, straight head, crested neck, compact body, powerful hindquarters, strong legs
colour predominantly white-grey, occasionally brown, black
height 15–16 hands
uses High School, dressage, harness

Vienna's 'dancing white horses' have a long and proud history – the Lipizzaner is thought to be the oldest European breed, having begun in 1580 at a stud founded by Archduke Charles II, son of the Austrian emperor Ferdinand I.

The archduke was tasked with establishing a stud to provide the Austrian court with fine horses for both riding and carriage driving, and he chose a derelict village near Trieste called Lipizza (now Lipica) in which to establish his breeding base, using 24 mares and nine stallions from Spain. These were a mixture of Andalucians and Barbs, which he crossed with local Karst horses. The Karsts were white, small of stature and slow to mature, but tough and energetic, with a high-stepping flashy gait.

The modern Lipizzaner traces back to six foundation sires: the grey Pluto (foaled 1675), of pure Spanish breeding; Conversano (1767), a black Neapolitan; the white Maestoso (1773) and dun Favory (1779), both Kladrubers; Neapolitano (1790), another Neapolitan, as his name suggests, and a white purebred Arab, Siglavy (1810).

Mares are bred in 16 lines named for their ancestresses: Sardinia, Spadiglia, Argentina, Africa, Almerina, Presciana, Englanderua, Europa, Stornella, Famosa, Deflorata, Gidrana, Djerbin, Mercurio, Theodorasta and Rebecca.

During its tumultuous history, the Lipizzaner stud has been moved several times – at one point it was owned by Napoleon, who introduced Arab bloodlines – and various military offensives almost threatened the breed's existence. In the early 20th century, there were just 208 pure Lipizzaners left. The breed was again on the brink of extinction during World War II, when forced to move by the German High Command, but was saved by the Spanish Riding School's then director, Alois Podhajsky.

The stud is now located at Piber, a tiny village in the Styrian Mountains, lower Austria, having been moved there in 1920. These magnificent horses are almost always white, with foals being born dark brown or black and lightening as they mature. Some do stay the darker colours, however, and it is a long tradition that there is always a brown or black horse resident at the Riding School.

Today, there are about 3,000 Lipizzaners, the best of which can be seen dancing in the baroque glory of the Spanish Riding School of Vienna. Here they perform the magnificent 'airs above the ground', spectacular feats of horsemanship that illustrate true harmony between horse and rider.

To see these mighty stallions perform in their Viennese home is unforgettable, but the Lipizzaner is also gaining in popularity as a dressage horse, due to the suppleness and athleticism he has inherited from his ancestors.

'The best of the breed can be seen dancing in the baroque glory of the Spanish Riding School of Vienna.'

Maremmano

conformation plain, coarse head, short neck, weak
    shoulders, strong hocks, hard feet
colour bay, brown, black
height 16 hands
uses cavalry, police, agriculture, light draught

Until relatively recently, Tuscany's native breed was considered of little value, although the horse was tough and courageous. He takes his name from the Maremma coast, a region of low marshland, and was used by both the Italian cavalry and the Butteri – Italy's version of the cowboy. The Butteri ride the Maremmano horses in a special saddle called a *bardella* or *scafarda*, the latter similar to the military saddle with a high arch and a padded seat. In the best cowboy tradition, the riders hold both reins in one hand and in the other an *uncino*, a shaped stick to help them in their job. A well-trained Maremmano can sprint from a standstill, stop and change direction quickly and precisely.

The job of the Butteri was to herd the buffalo and Maremman cattle of the region. With the draining of the marshes and the increasing cultivation of the area, many herds – and, with them, the Butteri – moved north, recreating their world around Grosseto, which became the capital of the Maremma region.

Today, the Butteri still use the horses in rounding up and branding the young cattle of the last remaining farms of the region, likewise the young Maremmanos, which are allowed to roam in a semi-feral state until the age of three or four, when they are herded into narrow enclosures and isolated for breaking in.

The horse himself hardly fills the eye – he is plain and somewhat coarse, although Arab, Barb, Norfolk Trotter and Thoroughbred blood has refined him to a degree, so that his profile is usually more straight than convex and his head smaller. It is thought that he descended originally from Neapolitan horses, although some speculate that he goes back even further, to Przewalski's Horse (see page 10) and the Sorraia of Iberia.

Today's Maremmano is still an honest, sturdy, hard worker and is used by the mounted police as well as the cavalry. He is a good doer and of calm and measured temperament, which keeps him in demand for riding and farm work. As Tuscany becomes an increasingly popular holiday destination, her indigenous horses are being used as trekking mounts.

But perhaps the Maremmano's heart remains with the Butteri, although increasing mechanization and cultivation means that most Italian cowboys now only demonstrate their spectacular skills in fairs and displays. As an old Tuscan poem goes: 'Put a saddle on the last horse / I want to go away from this land.'

'A well-trained Maremmano can sprint from a standstill, stop and change direction quickly and precisely.'

Landais

conformation neat head, thickset neck, straight back, muscled legs, high-set tail
colour bay, brown, chestnut, black
height 11–13 hands
uses riding, harness

One of the three breeds native to France, the Landais is a neat, good-looking pony, the result of infusions of Arab, Anglo-Arab and Barb blood – indeed, he is said to resemble a miniature Arab. He originates from southwest France and is sometimes referred to as the Barthais, which was once a separate breed. The Barthais was slightly bigger and heavier, but it is not known when the two breeds merged.

The Landais dates back to at least the early 8th century and the Eastern blood was probably introduced around the time of the Battle of Poitiers in AD 732. Later, there may have been some Spanish influence on the breed. In the early 20th century breeders added more Arab blood, but the Landais declined severely during World War II and breeders, trying to avoid too much inbreeding, were forced to add further outcrosses, including the Welsh pony.

Today's Landais is an elegant riding pony type with athletic paces, a good jump and an amenable temperament, although he can be somewhat wilful. A studbook was established in 1975 and he is officially recognized as being 'potentially endangered', with perhaps less than one hundred purebreds remaining.

Murgese

conformation attractive, convex head, upright shoulders, flat withers, clean, strong legs
colour chestnut, black, grey
height 15–16 hands
uses light draught, riding

A rare breed, the Murgese takes his name from the area of Murge, Apulia, in Italy. The breed is thought to be about 600 years old, and was usually black in colour, although grey also occurs, a throwback to his oriental ancestors. The region from which he originated is cold in winter and hot and dry in summer, and its horse is hardy and adapted to his natural habitat. His strong, sound legs and hard feet make him suited to the rocky limestone hills, and he is agile and surefooted. In the 15th and 16th centuries he found favour as a cavalry horse, but interest in him later waned and the breed was almost wiped out. It enjoyed a revival in the early 20th century, but today the Murgese probably bears little relation to his ancestors.

The introduction of Thoroughbred blood has produced a lighter, inferior version of something like an Irish Draught, although the Murgese is a tough, sweet-natured equine that makes a good all-round riding horse and, renowned as a good doer, is economic to keep. Chestnut is now the most usual colour, although the old blacks still appear. Murgese mares are good breeders and produce the tough mules still worked in the Murge region.

Noriker

conformation handsome head, defined withers,
    strong shoulders, deep body, good, sound feet
colour all solid colours, particularly liver chestnut with
    flaxen mane and tail, also spotted
height 16–17 hands
uses draught, riding, harness

The Noriker is a gentle giant, a coldblooded draught type that dates back to around 600 BC and takes his name from the Roman province of Noricum – he is sometimes called the Noric Horse – in what is now Austria.

The breed reached the height of its popularity in the 8th century. Frescos in the city's renowned Pferdeschwamme (horse pool) depict a heavy, Roman-nosed equine, almost certainly of coldblooded origin. Other portrayals from around that era show the Noriker in a range of extravagant colours and markings, called variously 'tiger', 'leopard' and 'isabel' – this last being an alternative name for palomino.

The Salzburg archdiocese's breeding programme adhered to strict guidelines and the resulting animals were much in demand for ceremonies and parades. In an attempt to produce a lighter riding type of horse, Neopolitan and Andalucian blood was introduced, which was not universally popular. The horse was still vital to the alpine farmers, and it is believed that some of them hid Noric stallions for breeding on their own mares.

At one time there were several recognized strains of Noriker, but of these the purest was the Pinzgau, named for the region, which included Pangau and Lungau. The Pinzgauer Noriker was later used as a prototype on which to re-establish the modern breed, with Clydesdale, Holstein and Belgian blood.

The modern Noriker bears a marked resemblance to the Belgian coldblood, although he has considerably more quality and spirit than most heavy draught types. He is most generally chestnut in colour, although bays, blacks, roans and leopard spots are still occasionally seen.

Freiberger (Franches-Montagnes)

conformation small, pony-like head, short neck, compact
    body, powerful hindquarters, strong legs
colour all solid colours
height 14.3–15 hands
uses harness, packhorse, agriculture

Originating in the Jura Mountains in Switzerland, the
Freiberger – also called the Franches-Montagnes – is said to
be Switzerland's only indigenous horse breed. He is a strong
and hardy light draught horse, agile, robust and surefooted.
He was of great value to the Swiss army, being used to
transport both men and equipment through the mountains,
and to the farmers, some of whom still use him today to work
fields that are too steep for tractors.

    Like the Einsiedler, he is based on Norman stock. Many
modern Freibergers can be traced back to one stallion,
Vaillant (1891), who was a great-grandson of an English
hunter with Norfolk Trotter blood called Leo I. Highly valued
in his homeland, the horse's breeding is government
controlled, the state stud being based at Avenches, and
retains the Anglo-Norman lines. In the past 150 years or so
some Thoroughbred blood has been added, making an active
little horse combining good looks, endurance and stamina.
He is a chunky little creature with a neat, pony head and
powerful hindquarters, and his character is both docile and
energetic. More recently he has been crossed with a Shagya
Arab to produce a new breed, the Freiberg Saddle Horse.

'He is a chunky little creature with a neat,
pony head and powerful hindquarters.'

Pindos

conformation small, straight head, strong neck, sloping
shoulders, deep girth, small, hard feet
colour black, bay, grey, occasionally roan
height 13–14 hands
uses agriculture, pack pony, riding, harness

Greece's smallest pony breed originates from the river valley of Pinios, in the Peloponnese. Little is known about this ancient mountain equine other than that he is probably descended from oriental bloodlines, with Arab and possibly some Thoroughbred blood. Some animals have light-coloured manes and tails, perhaps the result of an experiment with Haflinger outcrosses that failed dismally, the resulting animal being less hardy but with no added benefits.

The Pindos is an exceptionally tough little creature, agile and surefooted, with hard feet and sound constitution. The mountain terrain is hazardous and unforgiving, the summers blisteringly hot and the winters harsh, with temperatures still as low as -13°C (9°F) in early spring, but the Pindos has adjusted to these conditions. Despite his small size, the Pindos is strong enough to carry a man. Pindos mares are bred to donkeys to produce mules, which are enduring and even cheaper to keep.

What is considered to be a subspecies of the Pindos exists today as an endangered wild herd on the island of Kefalonia, which lies off the west coast of Greece. Known as Ainos Horses, named for the island's Mount Ainos – the third highest mountain in Greece at 1,570 m (5,100 ft) – there are just 22 left.

Pottok

conformation medium head, sometimes dished, short neck,
   slightly sloping shoulders, lean, strong legs, hard feet
colour all colours, including skewbald and piebald,
   except grey
height 11.2–14 hands
uses riding, harness, dressage, cross-country, endurance

For millennia, a wild herd has roamed the Basque region of southwest France – prehistoric cave drawings in the area depict small wild equines – but little is known about the Pottok's origins. He is thought to be related to the primitive Tarpan, although certainly Arab and Welsh blood has been introduced – many Pottoks have a distinctive dished face.

Robust and nimble, he is a hardy equine – a small horse, rather than a pony – that was used in agriculture and mining, as well as in the smuggling trade between France and Spain. He is also believed to be the basis for the coloured Mustangs of North America, taken by the Spanish conquistadors as packhorses, and the foundation stock for the ponies of Chincoteague Island.

A studbook was established in 1970 with two sections – Pottok A, for purebreds, and Pottok B, for mares crossed with Arabs or Welsh Ponies. Most studbook A ponies continue to live wild in the Basque mountains, being rounded up annually and a proportion sold.

The Pottok is sweet-natured and very athletic, particularly those of studbook B, which make a superb child's mount.

Salernitano

conformation light, fine head, long, muscular neck, well-proportioned back, good legs with plenty of bone
colour bay, chestnut, black, grey
height 16–17 hands
uses competition

The Salernitano is Italy's sports horse, an athletic, attractive equine with a natural bold jump and a high tolerance of hot weather (the breed is thought to have its origins in the Mediterranean island of Sicily). How or when the horses made their way to mainland Italy is not known, although the island may have once been connected to it. The horses are probably based on the Neapolitan, plus Spanish and oriental blood.

The first recorded Salernitano stud was at Persano, in southern Italy, founded by King Charles III in 1763 – the breed is sometimes called the Salernitano-Persano. Originally bred as a cavalry mount, it was the official horse of the Italian army until 1947.

The military was keen to compete in equestrian sports and made its cavalry mounts available to the soldiers, thereby increasing the Salernitano's popularity as a sports horse. The Italian army showjumping squad competed mostly on Salernitanos and was one of the best teams in the world from the end of World War II until the 1970s.

In the 20th century, Thoroughbred blood was introduced to refine the breed further and the modern Salernitano makes a good all-round competition horse.

Sardinian

conformation attractive, intelligent head, graceful neck,
  well-proportioned body, sound legs and feet
colour all solid colours
height 15.2 hands
uses competition, racehorse

Sardinia's only native breed is something of an enigma. Although the people of the Mediterranean island had for centuries used and bred their horses, little is known about the Sardinian's origins. He did, however, make an excellent military mount, and in 1874 a stud was founded at Ozieri, in northwest Sardinia, to promote and unify the breed. The horse was thought to have a particular affinity to the French-bred Anglo-Arab, and in 1883 several Anglo-Arabs were imported and bred to existing Sardinian horses. In 1915 more oriental blood was added, producing an agile and sturdy horse much desired by the military.

The next milestone in the Sardinian horse's history was the opening of the racecourse at Chilivani in 1921, which ignited great passion for horseracing on the island. To give the native breed increased speed, Thoroughbred blood was introduced. This was far from universally popular, with great debate about the virtues of the *Arabismi* (Arab) and the *purosanguisti* (Thoroughbred). The speed merchants won their case and a Thoroughbred stallion, Rigolo, was introduced in 1937. He was followed by a further three – Zenith, Sambor and Abimelecco. The superlative athlete that resulted became known as the Sardinian Arabic English horse, the breeding of which is still carefully guarded today.

'*Little is known about the Sardinian's origins, making him something of an enigma.*'

Skyros

conformation small, neat head, straight shoulders,
   narrow body, small feet
colour bay, dun
height 9.1–11 hands
uses agriculture, packhorse

A race is on to save this breed of pony, which exists only on the Greek island of Skyros, the largest and most remote of the Sporades Islands. No one knows how long these ponies have existed, although some believe they are the little equines depicted on the frieze of the Parthenon.

The pony resembles a scaled-down version of England's Exmoor pony, displaying the same mealy muzzle and prominent 'toad' eye.

Skyros is an island of two halves, the north side fertile and lush, the south more mountainous and less hospitable. During the summer months the ponies lived in the mountainous south, but as winter approached they migrated north in search of food and water, and apparently allowed themselves to be captured by farmers and used for threshing and other vital agricultural work.

However, in the mid-20th century, as increased mechanization changed the face of farming and European Union grants encouraged farmers to keep livestock, such as sheep and goats, the Skyros pony became redundant and his mountain habitat increasingly overgrazed. It is believed there are now less than 140 ponies left on the island – Skyros law does not permit their export – and these are possibly not all purebreds.

Einsiedler

conformation good-looking head, muscular neck, strong
   body, powerful hindquarters, long, hard legs, good feet
colour all solid colours, but predominantly chestnut, bay
height 16–16.2 hands
uses riding, competition, harness

Throughout history, the monasteries of the Western world have played an important role in horse breeding. Switzerland's own warmblood – the result of crossing a coldblood, such as a heavy draught type, with a hotblood, Arabian or Thoroughbred – is no exception.

The breed, sometimes also referred to as the Swiss Anglo-Norman or Swiss Half-Bred, is thought to have been in existence since the 10th century and remains a highly desirable dual-purpose equine. He takes his name from the Benedictine Abbey of Einsiedeln, where it is believed the breed was first established.

Perhaps influenced by the Holstein, Selle Français and Hanoverian, with Thoroughbred blood somewhere in his lineage, the Swiss version is a durable horse of great beauty and character. He stands upwards of 16 hands, and combines generally good conformation and an easy-going nature with athleticism and physical strength. He is found in all solid colours, including palomino and roan.

Previously in demand as a cavalry mount, the modern Swiss warmblood – which undergoes performance testing in his homeland – is in great demand as a competition horse, where he shines in most equestrian disciplines and also makes an impressive carriage horse.

Groningen

conformation convex head, short neck, long back, broad, strong hindquarters, round joints
colour black, bay, brown
height 15.2–16.2 hands
uses agriculture, harness

This powerful horse is somewhere between a warmblood and a draught type, a massive and imposing equine that combines strength and presence. He is bigger and heavier than his native cousin, the Dutch Warmblood, to whom he bears a resemblance, but as recently as 1985 a studbook was established to prevent the Groningen being absorbed into the latter and to maintain the two distinct breeds. The studbook's objective is to preserve and protect 'a heavy warmblood

horse with a powerful musculature, an appealing head, a strong and well-carried neck, good withers, a wide and deep rump, solid bones, short and strong cannon bones and wide, hard feet'.

In 1970 the breed was nearing extinction, with only one purebred stallion remaining, called Baldewijn. Oldenburg blood has since been introduced to improve the Groningen and to avoid inbreeding. Experiments with Holstein and even Cleveland Bay stallions produced too much diversity, the breed losing its characteristics. Later, both Thoroughbred and Trakehner blood was used to keep the Groningen breed going without compromising it. There are only about 300 Groningens left; every year in August the breed has its own national show, during which horses put through in regional selections go forward for final approval.

Holstein

conformation elegant head with large, expressive eyes, set on a fine, arched neck, well-proportioned body, good legs
colour bay, few or no white markings
height 16–17 hands
uses competition, harness

The Holstein is the product of systematic breeding dating back to the 13th century, when Gerhard, Count of Holstein and Storman, bestowed grazing rights on the monastery at Uetersen. The monks continued to breed fine horses until the Reformation, when monastery properties were transferred to private landowners, who continued the work begun by the monks. Great pride was taken in selecting the best bloodlines and keeping detailed breeding records.

The Holstein was based on Neapolitan, Spanish and oriental blood, crossed with the heavier native stock. The resulting horse was valued by the farmers and landowners for his strength and dependability, and by the cavalry for his courage and stamina. In 1686, laws were passed and incentives were offered to ensure the breed retained its quality. The Holstein's reputation soared through the 17th and 18th centuries – in 1797 alone, 10,000 were exported.

As the need for warhorses declined in the 19th century, English Cleveland Bay and Yorkshire Coach Horse blood was introduced and the breed evolved into a smart, high-stepping carriage horse. After World War II, Thoroughbreds were used for further refinement and to increase jumping ability – and the Holstein became the great German sports horse of today, as well as being influential in the development of other warmblood breeds.

Hanoverian

conformation plain, straight head, long, strong neck,
   powerful body with deep girth, strong hindquarters,
   good bone
colour all solid colours
height 15.3–17 hands
uses riding, competition

Perhaps Germany's most famous equine export and the best known of the European warmbloods, the Hanoverian excels in every equestrian discipline, be it dressage, three-day eventing or showjumping. An all-round athlete, he combines strength and grace, elegance and elasticity, speed and endurance, calmness and courage.

The breed originated in northern Germany in the province of Lower Saxony, formerly the kingdom of Hanover, where a thriving horse-breeding industry had existed for hundreds of years. In 1735, the state stud was established at Celle by George II, Elector of Hanover and King of England, with 14 black Holstein foundation stallions. The Hanoverian studbook was officially started in 1888.

Domestic German stock was bred to Thoroughbred stallions to add height and quality for both the military and the farming industry. The resulting equines made superb warhorses, possessing both courage and trainability, as well as a level-headed and calm temperament. As the need for cavalry mounts declined, the emphasis was placed on producing a versatile and superior performance horse, and Arab and Trakehner blood was added, as well as further infusions of Thoroughbred.

The breed retains the substantial bone, sturdiness and stamina of its forefathers, but the modern Hanoverian has more natural impulsion and light and elastic gaits, characterized by a good, ground-covering walk, a floating trot and a soft, round, rhythmic canter. Refinement of the horse has not taken away his equable and sensible temperament, his intelligence or his willingness. Today he is revered and coveted the whole world over.

Continued breeding of this superb horse is closely monitored, with only approved and graded stallions being used. All stallions must be presented for physical inspection, and are granted a temporary breeding licence only if they score sufficiently highly on conformation, movement and jumping ability. Within two years, stallions must complete and pass the 100-day stallion performance test that evaluates gaits, trainability and athletic ability in dressage, showjumping and cross-country. Eligibility for breeding is verified annually. Mares are also tested, from the age of 2½ years on, when they are evaluated on type, conformation and movement. Stallions must have a distinctly masculine bearing and mares a marked feminine expression.

All Hanoverians are branded on their near hindquarters with the distinctive 'H' – modelled on the crossed horses' heads at the gable of the breeding studs in Lower Saxony.

'He excels in every discipline, from dressage to showjumping.'

Oldenburg

conformation fine, noble head, good neck, sloping
   shoulders, muscular hindquarters, good legs, hard feet
colour predominantly black, brown, grey
height 16–16.3 hands
uses competition, harness

Originally bred as a coach horse, the powerful Oldenburg is today as much in demand as a competition animal as his close neighbour, the Hanoverian. The former kingdom of Oldenburg is a tiny region of Lower Saxony, surrounding the city of the same name in the centre of Hanover, but although it may be the smallest breeding area in Germany it is nevertheless one of the most important.

It is thought the breed was established by Herzog Anton Gunther von Oldenburg – a renowned horseman of the day – in the 17th century, based on Friesian horses and using Neapolitan, Turkish, Spanish and Barb blood. The early Oldenburgs were consistent in conformation and possessed great power, which, combined with their regal black colour, made them hugely popular as carriage horses. They were also famed for their kind character and willingness to work, either in harness or under saddle.

In 1820, the state decreed that all stallions be subject to testing and approval; a register of pedigrees was established in 1861 and two horse-breeding societies were founded under the Horse-Breeding Act of 1897. The two societies later merged into one.

As the demand for carriage horses gradually receded, Thoroughbred blood was added to produce a lighter, more elegant breed, although the Oldenburg is still the heaviest of all German warmbloods. Three stallions were initially used to refine him – the Thoroughbred Lupus XX, winner of the 1935 Derby; Condor (1950), an Anglo-Norman horse with 62.5 per cent Thoroughbred blood; and Adonis XX (1959) – and later still French blood was introduced, including the renowned Anglo-Norman sire Furioso.

By combining these various bloodlines with the traditonal Oldenburg mares, in a relatively short period of time breeders produced an equine that now belongs in the top echelon of modern sports horse breeds.

Today's Oldenburg is a handsome, large-framed and correct creature, with dynamic, elastic movement – well suited to dressage, showjumping or eventing – combined with proud bearing, calm temperament, kind character and rideability. Although still a big horse, he has a compact frame, noble head and neck well set on good withers and sloping shoulders, and a well-muscled topline. He carries himself well, pushing from his hocks and powerful hindquarters for energetic, forward-going gaits with active, long strides, as well as having a swinging back and good freedom of the shoulder. In short, he is poetry in motion, in whatever arena he competes.

'The Oldenburg is the heaviest of all the German Warmbloods.'

Selle Français

conformation attractive head, long neck, sloping
    shoulders, deep chest, long body
colour all solid colours
height 15.2–17 hands
uses competition, riding

One of the most modern warmbloods, the Selle Français was developed in the 19th century around the government stud farms of Saint Lô and Le Pin in the French region of Normandy. Breeders brought in English Thoroughbreds and Norfolk Trotters to cross with their native stock, producing two distinct types: the French Trotter, which was exceptionally fast in harness, and the Anglo-Norman. The Anglo-Norman was also developed in two different strains: a heavier draught type and the lighter, finer saddle type, the latter forming the basis of the Selle Français. The first Thoroughbred used was probably the curiously named Orange Peel, who stood at the Saint Lô Stud from 1925 to 1940, and whose grandson Ibrahim had enormous influence on the breed.

It was further developed using other native French horses, including Angevin and Angonin, Charentois, Charollais, Corlais, Limousin and Vendeen, and more Thoroughbred was also added, as well as some Anglo-Arab and Arab blood. The resulting mixture gradually became uniform and merged into one distinct breed, which was to be christened Le Cheval de Selle Français – the French Saddle Horse – in 1958, with a studbook established in 1965.

Today's Selle Français epitomizes everything desirable in a modern competition horse, combining good looks with superb paces and ability. He has extraordinary natural jumping talent – the Selle Français stallion Baloubet Du Rouet (a grandson of Ibrahim) won three consecutive World Showjumping Championships (1998–2000), as well as a silver medal in the 2004 Athens Olympic Games. In the 2002 World Equestrian Games in Jerez, Spain, the French team took showjumping gold, all mounted on Selle Français stallions.

But he does not only excel in the showjumping arena: France's star also shines in dressage and three-day eventing, and his speed makes him a superb racehorse in his native land under the rules of the AQPSA – Autres que pur Sang Association, meaning 'other than Thoroughbred'.

Today, the Selle Français continues to be an amalgamation of breeds, with 33 per cent by Thoroughbred sires, 20 per cent by Anglo-Arab, 2 per cent by French Trotter and 45 per cent by Selle Français stallions. He remains a handsome animal, intelligent and tractable by nature, with an almost doglike eagerness to please, which makes him highly trainable for any equestrian sphere.

'The Selle Français has an extraordinary jumping talent.'

Trakehner

conformation refined head, tapering neck, sloping
   shoulders, well-proportioned body, hard legs
colour all solid colours
height 16–17 hands
uses competition, riding

One of the oldest of the European warmbloods, the Trakehner is of East Prussian origin and named for the world-famous stud farm of Trakehnen, where the breed was established in 1732. The stud was opened by King Frederick Wilhelm I of Prussia, who required his cavalry to have a reliable means of transport that was faster, sounder and tougher than that of his enemies. He also wanted the mounts to be handsome, so his soldiers would be proud to ride them.

The foundation stock was the small native mares, called Schwaike, which were crossed with Thoroughbreds and purebred Arabs. The Schwaike horses possessed great speed and versatility, and crossing them with the hotbloods produced a fast and willing warhorse.

In 1787 the stud was taken over by Count Lindenau, who, determined to improve the breed further, eliminated one-third of the broodmares and two-thirds of the stallions, and the first studbook was opened in 1877. Trakehner breeding has been strictly monitored since then, with further Thoroughbred and Arab blood added only when deemed absolutely necessary and under stringent approval. The breed thrived and gained world renown, winning gold medals in dressage and eventing at successive Olympics, and also winning the terrifying and testing Pardubika Steeplechase, in what was then Czechslovakia, a total of nine times in 15 years.

Breed numbers were halved by World War I but recovered swiftly; it was World War II that was almost to bring about its demise. As Russian forces closed in at the end of the war, some 800 of the best horses were evacuated from the Trakehnen Stud, but did not get far. They were subsequently shipped to Russia and allowed to leave only in January 1945, when what is now known as The Trek saw the East Prussians load up their horses with their belongings and make the hazardous and arduous journey back to their homeland. Only about 100 horses survived.

The next decade was spend re-establishing the Trakehner, with a new studbook – the West German Trakehner Verband – being opened in 1947. Existing Trakehner horses were painstakingly tracked down and the breed was slowly revived, without being compromised. No outside blood other than Thoroughbred or Arab was permitted, and the resulting equines were to form the basis for other European breeds such as the Hanoverian and Westphalian.

Today's Trakehner is one of the biggest success stories of modern horse breeding, and of triumph over almost unimaginable hardship.

'No outside blood other than Thoroughbred or Arab was permitted.'

Westphalian

conformation intelligent head, well-shaped neck, deep,
 broad body, powerful hindquarters, good legs
colour all solid colours
height 15.3–16.2 hands
uses competion, riding

To all intents and purposes, the Westphalian is a Hanoverian, bred in the German region of Westphalia. It is thought to be based on feral horses living in the area that date back to Roman times, surviving in marshy areas unsuitable for agriculture. Five of these wild herds continued into the 19th century, and the last still exists today near Duelmen, where the annual round-up of young stallions is a popular spectacle.

The state stud – *Landgestuet* – was founded in 1826 at Warendorf, and the Westphalian Breed Registry was opened in Münster in March 1904. Early Westphalian horses were bred using Oldenburg and Anglo-Norman stallions, but since 1920 the Westphalian has been based on Hanoverian blood.

The goal was to breed an all-round riding and competition horse that was both beautiful and practical. Hanoverian blood is still used, but Thoroughbred and Trakehner lines have also been introduced, resulting in a lighter, finer equine of kind character and temperament, which excels in the dressage and showjumping arenas.

Perhaps the most famous Westphalian is the great Rembrandt, who won four Olympic dressage gold medals in the Games of 1988 and 1992.

Wielkopolski

conformation quality head, deep, powerful body,
    muscular hindquarters, strong legs
colour all solid colours
height 16 hands
uses riding, harness

Poland's only breed of warmblood is perhaps the least well known and was developed only about 40 years ago. He was bred as a riding and driving horse in west-central Poland in 1964, using the Mazury and Poznan breeds, both of which are now extinct. The Mazury was similar to the Trakehner, while the Poznan comprised a combination of Arab, Hanoverian and Thoroughbred blood. All Polish warmbloods are now known as the Wielkopolski, although for some time there

were two distinct types and the breed is sometimes still referred to as the Mazursko-Poznanski. Continued selective breeding has merged the two types into one.

This horse is undeniably handsome – with a fine, intelligent head, strapping, well-proportioned body and notably powerful hindquarters. As well as being a superb carriage horse – and Poland's successful driving competitors invariably use Wielkopolski horses – he has a good jump and natural athletic ability. He also has excellent balance and pleasing paces, including a long, loose walk, low, level trot and a ground-covering canter and gallop, making him suitable for the dressage arena.

Today, all Wielkopolskis born at the national stud have a numerical brand under the saddle, while foals from private regional breeders are branded on the near thigh.

British Warmblood

conformation good-looking head, medium-length neck, sloping shoulders, deep girth, long, clean legs
colour all solid colours
height 15.2–16.2 hands
uses competition

Given the almost unmatched success of the English Thoroughbred, it is perhaps surprising that Britain's own warmblood horse is a fairly recent development. Yet of all the world's equines, the warmblood is perhaps the greatest modern success story, and Britain – which continues to lead the way in many aspects of equestrianism – has to be counted as part of it.

While the Cleveland Bay is sometimes referred to as the 'English Warmblood', Britain first began a warmblood-breeding programme in the 1960s, importing Hanoverian, Trakehner, Dutch and Danish stallions. Among the most important were the Dutch Warmblood Dutch Courage – who competed successfully in dressage with Jennie Loriston-Clarke and became the foundation sire of her Catherston Stud – the Selle Français Dallas, who died in 2004, and the Danish Warmblood Baron B. Dutch Courage sired Dutch Gold, who represented Great Britain at Olympics and World Cup finals and became the only British-bred dressage horse to head the Nashua European League points table.

The British Warmblood Society was established in 1978, and the breed continues to impress – combining good looks, power, athleticism and energy with a sensible temperament. Like all warmbloods, the British version is stringently tested and only approved stallions are registered and accepted for breeding purposes. However, while warmbloods remain popular, more Thoroughbred quality is being introduced.

American Warmblood

conformation neat head, pleasing topline, deep chest, powerful hindquarters, good bone
colour all solid colours, but predominantly bay
height 16.1 hands
uses competition

America has enjoyed a long love affair with horseracing and boasts world-renowned Thoroughbred studs, but her sports horse is a comparatively new breed, and one that did not immediately enjoy the success of other warmbloods. In part, this was due to confusion about what a warmblood actually is – many thought it was the result of crossing any coldblooded horse with any hotblood, but this, of course, is not the case. The result of such a mating would be a 'draught-cross', or as the Americans themselves would put it, a 'mutt horse'. This confusion has occasionally led to the term American Warmblood being used in a derogatory way.

However, the true American Warmblood, like his European cousins, is a picture of equine perfection, possessing good looks, an even temperament and athletic ability. His gaits are elastic and athletic – his walk is straight and swinging; his trot easy and forward-going; his canter loose and free; his gallop long and ground-covering.

He is a noble, well-mannered and obedient horse, energetic and trainable. He is, indeed, a blend of the best of equine quality.

The American Warmblood Society was founded in 1983 to promote and improve America's newest breed and it looks set fair to continue the sports horse phenomenon.

Canadian Warmblood

conformation handsome head, good uphill topline, deep girth, clean, powerful legs, sound feet
colour all solid colours
height 16.2–17.1 hands
uses competition

He was born to jump – a sports horse in every sense of the word, Canada's own warmblood excels in all spheres. Canada has produced an equine that combines all the best features of the warmblood – the elasticity of movement, strong good looks and kind disposition.

Canadian Warmbloods tend to be bigger than some of the other warmblood breeds, perhaps because many of them are bred along Hanoverian and Holstein lines. A popular sire/grandsire in Canada is the Holstein G Ramiro Z, who had some of the best sports horse lines to pass on to his offspring.

The Canadian Warmblood Horse Breeders' Association was established in 1988 with the express aim of 'breeding and developing international calibre warmblood horses for Canadian riders... [and] promoting a healthy and vibrant horse industry overall'. The association offers approvals and inspections, as well as *keuring* – performance testing – and is able to provide an artificial insemination service with chilled or frozen semen.

The Canadian version follows the warmblood blueprint – a good all-round performance horse ideal for competition, which combines athletic, active paces with the aristocratic good looks and speed of the Thoroughbred and strength and power of his German forebears.

Belgian Warmblood

conformation attractive head, short neck, compact body,
    deep girth, strong clean legs
colour all solid colours
height 15.2–16.2 hands
uses primarily showjumping and eventing, but good
    all-round competition horse

He has been called 'Europe's best-kept secret', but now the secret is out. Belgium's sports horse, one of the newest of all warmbloods, has made his mark on the competition world in a comparatively short time. The breeding programme originated in the early 1950s in the area of Brabant, home of the heavy draught equine of that name, but the modern horse bears little relation to the coldblood breed, although there may be some common ancestry.

The lighter Belgian farm horse was bred to Gelderlanders to produce a heavyweight riding horse which, although strong and reliable, was not particularly athletic. Breeders introduced Holstein blood for power and Selle Français for beauty – the influence of the latter can be seen in the Belgian Warmblood's fine head.

Anglo-Arab, Dutch Warmblood and Thoroughbred blood was later added, creating a superb equine of great natural athleticism, correct conformation, reliable temperament and, perhaps most important, the ability to pass on these valuable characteristics to his offspring. The horses are monitored through 'keurings' – or approvals – and only the best are accepted into the studbook.

While the Belgian Warmblood is noted for his talent in showjumping and three-day eventing, he is increasingly making a name for himself in the dressage arena as well, and it appears that this tiny European country has produced a giant among equine athletes.

'One of the newest of all warmbloods, he has been called "Europe's best kept secret".'

Danish Warmblood

conformation handsome head, well-proportioned
    neck, strong shoulders, medium-length back,
    good, powerful legs
colour all solid colours
height 16.2 hands
uses competition

Denmark is one of the oldest kingdoms in the world and her own warmblood is one of the most successful sports horse breeds. The Danish peninsula has other horse breeds, including the draught-type Jutland, but the warmblood burst on to the world stage in the 1980s with Marzog, one of the most successful dressage horses of all time, ridden by Anne Grethe Tornblad. They brought an extraordinary grace and lightness to the discipline.

Like all the warmbloods, the Danish version is a superior sports horse, and not just in the dressage arena. He has also excelled in three-day eventing and showjumping, combining elastic paces with natural athleticism and an easy-going temperament. This is borne out by the Danish Warmblood stallion Lando, who took a showjumping silver medal in the Sydney Olympics, when nine competing nations had Danish Warmbloods on their teams.

The national breeding programme, the Dansk Varmblood Avisforbund, was established in Denmark in 1962, its stock being bred on Polish and Swedish lines, with input from Trakehners, Hanoverians and Holsteins.

The Danes are rightly proud of their superlative competition horse and he is rigorously monitored and stringently tested to ensure the breed remains at the top of every equestrian game.

Dutch Warmblood

conformation somewhat plain head, medium-length neck, well-defined withers, long back, good hocks
colour all solid colours
height 16 hands
uses competition, harness

This horse's roots are planted firmly in two areas of the Netherlands, Gelderland and Groningen, which produce two different types of performance horse that complement each other perfectly. The sandy soil of the Gelderland made for a lighter, finer horse, while the clay of the Groningen region gave rise to a heavier, denser type. Subsequently, Gelderland horses were used to lighten the Groningen version, which in turn was used to add substance to the former.

The farmers of the Netherlands relied on their horses and strove to eliminate any weaknesses or faults, the resulting equine being sound, intelligent and conformationally strong. With the rise of mechanization, emphasis in breeding changed – keeping the soundness and intelligence, but adding more Thoroughbred blood to refine the horse and add quality. French, Holstein and Hanoverian blood was also added, and Hackney lines introduced to produce a striking harness horse.

The Dutch studbook is divided into three – sports horse, harness horse and traditional Gelderland type, this last being vital to maintain the gene pool – but today the term Dutch Warmblood continues to epitomize the renowned equine athlete that has carried the flags of many nations to Olympic glory.

Swedish Warmblood

conformation small, neat head, straight neck, compact
    body, rounded hindquarters, strong legs
colour all solid colours
height 15.2–16.3 hands
uses competition, harness

Archaeological evidence has been found for the existence of horses in what is now Sweden dating back to 4000 BC. The native horses were probably quite small, standing no higher than 14 hands, but were spirited and tough – desirable qualities that were to be retained. In 1661, King Carl X Gustaf developed a national stud farm in Flyinge to breed quality cavalry horses, and it is thought that Friesian horses were imported from Holland to add height to existing stock.

The stud's aim was to produce a horse of exceptional conformation, temperament, movement and versatility, and it certainly succeeded in its goal. At the first modern Olympiad, in 1912, Sweden took home three individual medals in dressage, and in the ensuing years Swedish horses have been in the medals at every Olympics, with the exception of Moscow in 1980, when many European countries boycotted the Games. In Seoul in 1988, six Swedish Warmbloods won medals.

In the 1970s, when it ceased to use horses, the army handed over control of the Flyinge stud to the Swedish Warmblood Association, which subjects its sports horse breed to strict inspection and approval processes to ensure it continues to excel at dressage, showjumping, three-day eventing and driving.

Døle/Døle Trotter

conformation pony head, crested neck, long back, short
    legs with dense bone, luxurious mane and tail
colour predominantly black, brown, bay, occasionally grey,
    dun, white markings permitted
height 14.2–15.2 hands
uses harness, packhorse

There were originally two types of the Døle breed: the Døle Trotter, a light harness horse with a fantastically energetic trot, and the heavier draught type, the Gudbransdal, a tough little creature used for agricultural work. Both types were coldblooded equines and are thought to have originated in the Gudbransdal Valley, which connects the Oslo area to the North Sea coast.

They bear similarities to the Friesian horse, and also to the English Fell and Dales ponies – the Friesian people were enthusiastic traders with Britain, Norway and the Rhine Delta in AD 400–800. One of the biggest influences on the Døle was the Thoroughbred stallion Odin – although sources variously describe him as a Norfolk Trotter – who was imported in 1834 to lighten the original coldblood. Some Arab blood was introduced by way of the stallion Dovre.

Today's Døle horses are increasingly merging into one, interbreeding ironing out the differences. However, the result is still an admirable harness horse – with a neat pony head, good, hard legs and feet, and a renowned turbo-charged trot. This is guarded closely: the National Dølehorse Association, established in 1967, will not permit breeding from stallions whose legs show defects on X-ray.

Finnish

conformation short head, upright shoulders, deep chest, strong hindquarters, strong, clean legs with light feathering
colour chestnut, bay, brown, black
height 14.2–15.3 hands
uses agriculture, harness, riding

Finland's only horse breed is sometimes referred to as the Finnish Universal because it is famed as a multi-purpose equine. This is a lightning-fast coldblooded trotter, an enduring harness horse capable of pulling heavier loads than many bigger draught types (while the average equine can pull up to 80 per cent of his own body weight, the Finnish can pull some 110 per cent) and a versatile riding horse that competes with the best in dressage, showjumping and cross-country. In addition, the horse has adapted to the harsh climate of his Scandinavian land and is long-lived. These attributes made him invaluable during times of war.

In 1924 the studbook was split into two: a heavier draught type for agriculture and forestry work, and the lighter riding type for trotting and racing. Later, four types developed – Type J, a lightly built horse; Type T, the heavy version; Type R, a versatile riding horse; and Type P, a smaller pony version. Most were chestnuts with a distinctive flaxen mane and tail, but today bays, browns and some blacks are also seen. Although most are still bred in Finland, some have been exported to Sweden and Germany, where the breed has a growing following.

'the Finnish can pull some 110 per cent of his own body weight'

Fjord

conformation pretty, straight or slightly concave head, small ears, short neck, powerful body, good legs and feet
colour all variations of dun, with lighter mane and tail, often a dorsal stripe
height 13.2–15 hands
uses riding, harness, packhorse

Look at cave paintings of some 30,000 years ago and you will see a creature that bears a remarkable resemblance to today's Fjord horse. It is thought he migrated to Norway, from whose famous waterways he takes his name, about 4,000 years ago. His origins are unknown, although many believe him to be closely related to the primitive Przewalski's Horse (see page 10), so it may be he came from the East, part of the wild herds found around Sweden and Denmark since the last Ice Age.

The Fjord does display the 'wild colour' of dun and all its variations, often including the dorsal stripe along the spine and zebra markings on the legs. His mane is also distinctive, with dark hairs in the centre and white to the outside, traditionally trimmed short so it stands erect, the dark stripe clearly visible down the length of his powerful neck. The whole impression is one of power but also grace – the Fjord is far from coarse, with a pretty head, compact, short-coupled body, strong legs and excellent feet. And his character is charm personified – he is gentle and willing and genuinely wants to please – which makes him an ideal equine for all the family.

Frederiksborg

conformation large head, upright neck and shoulders,
  flat withers, long legs
colour chestnut with flaxen mane and tail, white
  markings permitted
height 15.2–16 hands
uses harness, riding

Denmark's oldest breed is the horse of kings – literally. He was named for King Frederik II of Denmark, who founded a stud in the 1560s and imported horses from Italy and Spain to cross with native stock. The stud was highly successful and its horses greatly prized, as both cavalry mounts and carriage horses. By the 18th century, the stud was producing two discernible types – a riding horse with a beautiful, supple action, and a heavier, bigger horse for pulling the royal carriages. In this second type, it was important that the horses should be almost identical in size and colour so they could be driven in matched teams of six or even eight.

These handsome horses – which were used to form and improve other breeds – were exported in great numbers, with the breed going into decline in its native country. The royal stud closed in 1839. Fortunately, a number of private breeders retained their horses and in 1939 efforts were made to revitalize the breed, using Friesian and Oldenburg and, later, Thoroughbred and Arab blood.

The emphasis was placed on the riding type rather than the harness, but today the Frederiksborg, although a rare breed, continues to excel at both.

'Denmark's oldest breed was highly successful as both cavalry mount and carriage horse.'

Gotland

conformation elegant head, pronounced withers, long back,
    sloping hindquarters, hard feet
colour predominantly bay and dun, but all solid colours
    permitted except albino and roan
height 11.2–13 hands
uses harness, trotting, riding

There have been wild ponies on the Lojsta Moor, on the
Swedish island of Gotland, since the Stone Age. The Swedish
call him Russ but Gotlanders call the ponies *skogsbagga*,
which means 'little horse of the woods'. The oldest reference
to the Russ is found in Skånelagen, a legal code from the 13th
century, where 'the wild horses of Gotland' are mentioned.

The Gotland was captured and domesticated by the island
farmers and used for light draught work, but the changing
face of agriculture almost proved his downfall. In the early
19th century, small areas of the island were sold to individual
farmers, who fenced off the land and cultivated it. Because of
the damage they caused, the ponies that once were prized
came to be seen as pests.

Many Gotlands were exported to Belgium, Germany and
Britain – where they were used for mining – and numbers on
the island declined sharply. By the beginning of the 20th
century, only about 150 were left. The breed was saved and
allowed to run free, and has enjoyed a revival. There are
about 9,000 in Sweden and they can also be found in Finland,
Denmark and the United States.

Nordland

conformation plain head, thick mane and tail,
medium-length back, sloping croup, sturdy legs
colour chestnut, brown, bay, grey, but all solid colours
permitted except dun
height 12–13 hands
uses riding, harness, packhorse

Norway's native pony shows his Przewalski and Tarpan ancestry (see page 10) in his coarse head and stocky build, but he is conformationally sound and long-lived, often surviving to 30 years old and retaining fertility into advanced age. Despite his size, like the Icelandic (which he resembles) in Norway he is called a horse, not a pony.

He is thought to have arrived in Norway from the East, but for a number of reasons – perhaps in search of food –

ended up being concentrated in the northern region. He is variously referred to as Nordland, Northlands, Lyngen and Lyngshest, and there were at one time two distinct types, one from Lyngen in northern Troms, and one from Norland. The Lyngen type was bigger and heavier and predominantly chestnut, while the Norland type was smaller and finer, resembling the now extinct Lofoten Pony. Well-preserved finds from Viking graves suggest these horses were used in Norway long ago. Because of interbreeding between the two, today's Nordland is basically of one type and all solid colours are seen, with the exception of dun.

The Nordland was saved from extinction after World War II, and his equable temper, trainability and toughness make him a good packhorse. A willing and amicable worker that is not prone to any health problems, he also makes an excellent child's riding pony.

Icelandic

conformation neat head, sometimes double-sided mane,
    upright shoulder, short, strong legs, hard feet
colour all solid colours
height 12.3–13.2 hands
uses all-rounder

There is no Icelandic word for 'pony', so the country's only equine breed is called the Icelandic Horse, although he stands only 13–14 hands high. He has existed in Iceland since the 9th century, when conquering Vikings settled there, bringing with them their own horses, probably of German descent. Because of the isolation of the 'land of fire and ice', these horses were bred only to each other, producing a uniform and unique equine.

Arabian blood was introduced at one point, perhaps 900 years ago, but proved a disaster, having a detrimental effect on the breed. In AD 930, a law was passed by the Althing – the world's oldest Parliament – forbidding the use of outside blood on the Icelandic Horse.

The Icelandic was to play a vital role in his country's history, being the only means of transport and a vital working animal. He carried people over lava fields and mountains, and across the powerful glacier rivers. He was renowned as 'the most useful servant', literally following man from birth to death – bringing the doctor to the birth and pulling the coffin to the graveyard. When the first motor car was brought to Iceland in 1904, the country's native equine became largely redundant, but the Icelandic people are proud of their breed and ensured his survival – the first breed association was set up in the same year the car arrived.

Energetic, willing and trainable, the Icelandic Horse is one of the five-gaited breeds, possessing the lateral *tölt* – called the rack in America – a one-two-three-four beat gait that is fast and enormously comfortable for the rider. At the *tölt*, you cannot hear each foot set down; you hear only the front feet. At shows and displays, Icelandic Horses are often ridden at the *tölt* while the rider holds a full glass in one hand and the reins in the other, without spilling a drop.

The Icelandic Horse shows his primitive ancestry in his rather large but neat head, but is nonetheless an attractive creature, especially those whose double-sided manes contrast against their coats. He can be found in more than 40 different colours, with about 100 variations. He is slow to mature but is exceptionally long-lived, on average to 25–30 years old, but horses of 40 or more have been documented.

He has found favour outside Iceland, with about 100,000 being exported, mostly to Europe, although there are also Icelandic Horses in the United States and Canada. Today, there are about 80,000 horses in his homeland – not bad for a country with a human population of only 270,000.

Knabstrup

conformation small, refined head, medium length of rein, compact body, hard legs, strong feet
colour spotted
height 15.1–16 hands
uses riding, harness, circus

A Spanish officer imprisoned in Denmark during the Napoleonic Wars left behind his horse when he was granted his freedom. This horse, a chestnut mare with some white in her coat, was bought by a butcher called Flaebe, and the mare was to become known by the same name. She passed on her unusual colouring and sweet nature to her offspring. Bred initially to a yellow Frederiksborg stallion, she was to produce many progeny, but not one of them was a solid colour.

There are varying accounts of how the breed got its name. Some say the first were bred at Knabstrup Farm, but there is another, more interesting – and more romantic – suggestion. A man was injured by a carriage and urgently needed a doctor. A team of two horses was quickly harnessed and driven at speed to the nearest village of Holbaek, but no doctor was available, so the team hastened on to the next town, Buttrup, where it collected the doctor and transported him back at great pace to Knabstrup. The round trip of some 26 km (16 miles) was made in less than two hours – one horse was destroyed by the journey; the other soon recovered. This was the Flaebe mare.

Certainly, the Knabstrup horse is a robust and energetic creature. They were strong, too, and initially popular as military chargers, but their striking appearance made them all too easy a target on the battlefield. During the Battle of Isted in 1850, two Danish officers, both mounted on eyecatching Knabstrup horses, were shot. One horse, a mare called Nathalie, ridden by a Colonel Laessoee, was unharmed after the fall of her rider and was later bred from; one of her offspring was named Laessoee after the dead colonel.

The other horse, ridden by General Schleppegral, was a startling red spotted stallion. He was caught by local hill farmers in the region and kept hidden, but was used for breeding. The resulting progeny were known as Schnapegral-Peerd and were all strong, handsome equines of startling colour.

Almost inevitably, the breed went into decline, perhaps as a result of too much inbreeding, and suffered a loss of quality as breeders strove to keep the unusual colouring at the expense of conformation. The modern Knabstrup is a rare breed – and it would be a tragedy if it were lost completely.

'They were initially popular as military chargers, but their striking appearance made them too easy a target'

North Swedish

conformation large head, crested neck, strong back, short legs with plenty of bone

colour all colours

height 15.2 hands

uses harness, agriculture, forestry, riding

Like the Norwegian Døle, Sweden's coldblood is descended from the ancient Scandinavian native horse and is a versatile and enduring draught horse. He is lighter and finer than some coldbloods, but has their longevity and adaptability. He has an even temperament, which he combines with great energy, litheness and strength in relation to a comparatively small stature – mares are generally about 15 hands, while stallions stand about 15.2 hands.

In Sweden the horse probably reached its zenith in the early 20th century, when there were an estimated 720,000 adult equines in the country, some 80 per cent of which were the coldblooded draught. But with the increase in mechanization, the farm and forestry work for which the North Swedish horse was so ideally suited declined and so too did army requirements for cavalry and pack animals.

However, the North Swedish horse survived and today is bred in two distinct types, draught and trotters. The trotter has a particularly agile, springy action and is the world's only coldblooded harness racer. Both resistant to disease and economic to keep, he is also invaluable to farmers.

The main stud is at Wangen. The breed is subject to stringent testing to ensure that the North Swedish retains his endurance, longevity and supreme action.

RUSSIAN

Budenny (Budyonny)

conformation handsome, straight head, good length
of rein, deep girth, long legs, good bone
colour predominantly chestnut, but all solid colours
permitted
height 16–17 hands
uses competition

Russian hero Marshall Budenny is credited with founding
the breed that bears his name, following the Revolution (1917)
and the fall of the Tsar. He set out to produce an excellent
horse for the military to replace horses lost in World War I
and the protracted civil war, and bred Russian Don and
Chernomor mares with English Thoroughbreds. The breed
was for some time known as the Anglo-Don and was
predominantly chestnut, often with a glorious metallic sheen
attributed to the Don and, possibly, back to the Akhal-Teke.
The first official record of the breed was published in 1934.

Arabian blood was added to these Anglo-Dons, which
were then bred back to the Thoroughbred to develop an
elegant equine of tolerant disposition, stamina and
endurance. Of more than 70 Thoroughbreds used in Budenny
breeding between 1926 and 1940, only three stallions were
accepted into the studbook as its forefathers – Simpatyaga,
Inferno and Kokas. These three formed six major founding
lines: Simpatyaga's three sons, Sagib, Saksagan and Sagar;
Inferno's Imam and Islam; and Kokas's Kagul.

The Budenny was officially recognized as a breed in 1948,
ironically only a few years before the Russian cavalry was
officially disbanded in 1954.

Akhal-Teke

conformation fine, thin head, slightly dished, lean, high-set
neck, sloping shoulders, long back, clean legs
colour chestnut, bay, grey, palomino (isabella), black, dun,
all except black having an iridescent sheen
height 14.2–15.2 hands
uses riding, competition, endurance

Exotic and proud, this golden equine aristocrat has been revered for some 3,000 years – among his many fans were Alexander the Great and Genghis Khan, Roman emperors and Marco Polo. But he is not truly Russian in origin: he pre-dates the founding of the Soviet State by thousands of years. He actually comes from the Kara Kum Desert in Turkmenia, a testing place for the toughest people and the toughest equines. The Turkmene would never have survived without the Akhal-Teke and vice versa, and he takes his name from a Turkmenian tribe, Teke, that lived at the Akhal oasis.

This is a horse of great beauty – and great antiquity, older than the Arab. Images of the Akhal-Teke horse dated to the 9th century BC are found in the territory between the Caucasus and Luristan. To the Turkmene, he was invaluable – in the harsh desert, a good horse could mean the difference between life and death for his rider. The Kara Kum Desert occupied about 90 per cent of Turkmenistan, with no hope of survival for a horse unless he could tolerate extreme heat, dry cold and drought. Fresh grass was available for only a few months of the year; the domesticated Turkmene horse had to survive on meagre rations, generally high-protein grains mixed with animal fat.

In return, the tribesmen cared for their horses, feeding them by hand and blanketing them in the coldest weather – they were rightly proud of their beautiful equine partners. And to this day, the sensitive Akhal-Teke will bond closely with humans, although he can be stubborn.

The horses were first brought to Russia about 500 years ago, when they were known as Argamaks, meaning 'tall and refined'. Russia annexed Turkmenistan in the 1880s, and the first official Akhal-Teke stud, Zakaspiisky, was founded using the best stock. Among these was the stallion Boinou, forebear of some of the breeding lines used today.

The Akhal-Teke has influenced many modern breeds, including the Arab and the Thoroughbred – it is possible the Byerley Turk was an Akhal-Teke – as well as Russia's native breeds such as the Don and the Budenny.

The Akhal-Teke has often been given to heads of state as a gesture of goodwill. In 1956, Nikita Khrushchev presented Queen Elizabeth II with a stallion called Melekush. He was a magnificent golden dun with the breed's distinctive metallic sheen, so much so that the Queen's grooms spent some time trying to clean off what they thought was polish – the stallion's silky coat glowed all the brighter for the wash.

'images of the Akhal-Teke horse date to the 9th century BC'

Don

conformation straight head, lean neck, upright shoulders, broad back, hard legs
colour chestnut, bay, grey
height 16–16.2 hands
uses riding, competition, harness

The Don is Russia's oldest riding horse breed, taking his name from the Don River in the Russian steppes. Early Don horses were comparatively small and swift, making them a boon to the semi-nomadic people of the region: he was their willing partner in raids and skirmishes, and more than a match for their enemies' slower, heavier mounts. These nomads were runaway slaves and were called Kazak, a Mongolian word meaning 'armoured warrior on horseback'. They later became the Cossacks, revered and feared as Russian cavalrymen. Their horses, influenced by Karabakh, Persian and Turkmenic breeds, Arabs – perhaps introduced to the Cossacks' herds as war bounty – and the Thoroughbred, were also prized.

The first dedicated Don stud farms were established in the late 18th century, when more Arab and Karabakh blood was added to produce a bigger horse, although still refined. He was valued as an all-purpose military steed, but was almost wiped out at the beginning of the 20th century, when after World War I and the civil war only a few hundred remained. Since then, there has been a revival in the breed.

As well as being a riding and competition horse, the Don is popular in tourism, often being driven in the traditional *tachanka*, in which four horses are harnessed side by side.

Kabardin

conformation plain head, upright, loaded shoulders, straight
   back, slightly curved hindlegs, exceptionally hard feet
colour brown, bay, black
height 15–15.1 hands
uses riding, trekking, harness

Willing and nimble, the Kabardin is arguably the world's best mountain breed. Nature made him reliable, surefooted and undemanding; man made him obedient and brave.

He was bred by the mountain people of the North Caucasus from the 16th century using Persian, Karabakh and Turkmenistan strains. The best Kabardins are raised at the Karachai and Malka Studs, and he is sometimes called the Karachai Horse.

Following the Russian Revolution, the breed was divided into three different types: the 'basic' was the original rangy mountain horse; the 'oriental' finer and more elegant; the 'massive' a carriage horse type, with longer body and more bone. But all encompassed the best aspects of the breed.

The blood of the Kabardin has a heightened oxidizing capacity; his heart and lungs are efficient and strong. He can quickly accumulate fat to keep him going through leaner times and he is a horse of great stamina. In 1946, a performance test of Russian breeds was carried out in Moscow – a ride of 250 km (155 miles) with the last 2 km (1¼ miles) covered at a gallop. The winner was the Kabardin stallion Ali-Kadym; his time was 25 hours.

As breeder Dr Gerhard Willenbrink says: 'Everyone dreams to have a horse like this.'

Karabakh

conformation small head, strong neck, compact body,
    long, slender legs, low-set tail
colour chestnut, bay, dun
height 14 hands
uses racing, riding, harness

Originating in Nagorny Karabakh in Azerbaijan, between the Araks and Kura Rivers, the Karabakh – an ancient mountain saddle horse – has been in existence since the 5th century. The breed was developed from the native Azerbaijan stock crossed with Persians, Arabs and Turkmenians. The Arabian influence was most pronounced, and there are important similarities in appearance between the Karabakh and the Arab. Likewise the Akhal-Teke, from whom the Karabakh has inherited his gorgeous metallic sheen.

The Karabakh is hardy and loyal, as well as swift and agile, and like most mountain breeds he is a good doer, vital to his nomadic masters. Latterly, his swift turn of foot has made him a popular racehorse, with performance testing held on racecourses.

In recent times, however, numbers have dropped alarmingly, and it is thought that there are only about 130 purebred Karabakhs left, although efforts are being made to revitalize the breed and the horse is currently being bred at Agdam Stud. A horse found in Azerbaijan, called the Deliboz, is believed to have been developed from the Karabakh using Tersk blood – some regard it as a subspecies of the Karabakh – but it is slightly bigger and of less certain temperament. The Deliboz occasionally shows another distinctive feature: a peculiar lengthwise fold on the tongue, giving the impression of a forked tongue.

Orlov Trotter

conformation small head, long neck, straight shoulders, deep girth, powerful hindquarters
colour grey, black
height 15.2–17 hands
uses trotting, harness, riding

Russia's most famous breed is a massive horse of great strength and beauty. He was developed in the late 18th century by Count Alexei Orlov, who was instrumental in the assassination of Paul III, which brought Catherine the Great to the throne. In gratitude, the Tsarina presented the count with a generous parcel of land in the fertile steppe region of Voronezh in central Russia. Here, he founded the Khrenovsky Stud in 1775.

The count used Arab stallions on royal Spanish and Danish mares, as well as English Thoroughbreds, Friesians and other breeds. His aim was to produce a superior equine of speed and endurance. His most influential purchase for the breeding programme was a stallion called Smetanka, a silver-grey Arab with a long back and an extravagant, long-striding trot. Disappointingly, the stallion died young, and an autopsy revealed the reason for his unusually long back: an extra rib.

Count Orlov continued his breeding programme using a Smetanka son called Poltan, and in 1784 a grey colt named Bars I was born. Eleven of this stallion's sons were used at Khrenovsky, two of them being of particular influence: the black Liubeznyl I and the grey Lebed' I. All modern Orlov Trotters can be traced back to one of these stallions.

Russian Trotter

conformation fine head, long, straight neck, long,
  well-muscled back, flat croup
colour bay, black, chestnut
height 16 hands
uses light harness

For decades, the Orlov Trotter was unsurpassed in terms of speed and strength, and was the fastest trotter in Europe. But as the world got smaller, he was outpaced by the American Trotter (Standardbred). Not only was the American version a smaller, finer-boned horse, but his harness was less heavy and he was driven to a lightweight sulky, known as the *amerikanka*. Following the dramatic success of the 'incomer', the race was on to improve the existing breed.

And so, in the late 19th century, Orlov horses were crossed with the American Trotter, the resulting equine being markedly faster than the purebred Orlov but at the expense of the beauty, power and stamina that are the latter's hallmark.

For harness-racing enthusiasts, however, this was a sacrifice they were prepared to make – most of them, at any rate. There followed protracted and heated debate within both the breeding and racing fraternities, some pleading the case for greater speed at all costs, others outraged as what they saw as the 'contamination' of Russia's favourite equine.

The Russian Trotter was recognized as a separate breed in 1949, since when efforts have been made to improve it and iron out conformation defects. But speed the horse certainly possesses – the record for a 1,600 m (1 mile) trot is 1 minute 56.9 seconds.

Tersky

conformation straight head, deep chest, muscular
   hindquarters, hard legs, high-set tail
colour predominantly grey, occasionally bay, chestnut
height 14.3–15.1 hands
uses racing, endurance, competition, circus

The Tersky bears a close resemblance to the Arab, on which
the breed was founded in the 19th century, when a fine,
speedy cavalry mount was developed using Arabs and Anglo-
Arabs on Karabakh, Orlov, Persian and Turkmenian horses.
The resulting equine was willing, gentle and intelligent, and
became known as the Streletsky, for the Ukrainian farm
where he was established. Usually of a light silvery grey
colour, his looks were as aristocratic as his pedigree.

Although never produced in vast numbers, the horse was
popular with the army – which was to prove his undoing.
Streletsky horses were virtually wiped out during the bloody
civil war, but two breeding stallions survived: Tsenitel (born
1910) and Tsilindr (1911), both by the influential sire Tsenny.

Although a few purebred mares were subsequently
located, the gene pool was too small to resurrect the
Streletsky, and Don, Kabardin and Arabian blood was
introduced. The breeding progamme began in 1925 at the
Tersk Stud, for which the new breed was named. In 1941,
under threat of German invasion, the entire stock was
evacuated to west Kazakhstan – a journey of 900 km (565
miles) that lasted 21 days. Four years later, the horses were
brought back east, to Stavropol Farm in the northern
Caucasus, where the breed remains to this day.

Ukrainian (Russian) Saddle Horse

conformation well-proportioned head, long, straight neck,
    solid build, plenty of bone
colour black, bay, chestnut
height 16.2 hands
uses riding, competition

This most modern of horse breeds began after World War II at Ukraine studs using Hanoverian, Trakehner, Nonius, Furioso and, later, Thoroughbred lines. It was, in effect, a resurrection of the Russian Riding Horse, sometimes called the Orlov-Rostopchin, which had been popular in the mid-19th century as a superb dressage horse.

The Orlov-Rostopchin suffered severe setbacks during World War I, the subsequent revolution and World War II, after which some sources prematurely declared it extinct due to both conditions of war and a stud farm fire that took the lives of most mares and youngstock.

However, some survived, their unusual coal-black colouring making them immediately identifiable. Bred with similar existing stock, the breed enjoyed a revival, albeit a covert one and under a new name.

The Saddle Horse proved a natural in the dressage arena, with the USSR (as it was then) rising to international supremacy in the 1950s, battling only with the then West Germany for Olympic, World and European glory.

The breed had been restored and to a remarkably high quality, with performance testing and evaluation measures still in use today. In 1978, the breeding operation was moved to the Starozhilovsky State Stud and the Ministry of Agriculture relinquished control of it – a rare gesture to the dedicated horsemen who saved the Saddle Horse.

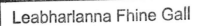

Australian Stock Horse

conformation intelligent head, sloping shoulders, high withers, strong back and hindquarters, hard feet
colour predominantly bay
height 15–16.2 hands
uses riding, competition

The Australian Stock Horse has been dubbed the 'breed for every need', praised for his versatility and superior performance among work and leisure horses.

Australia's equine history began with the arrival of the First Fleet, the ships bringing British convicts to the new colony in 1788. These first horses were Thoroughbreds and Spanish stock, and they had to be tough. If they were strong enough to survive the gruelling journey – which was thought to have lasted 9–12 months – they then had to possess the stamina to work and thrive in their strange, new, harsh and untamed environment.

As the settlers explored more of this strange new continent, they relied on their horses, which had to travel long distances, day after day. The weaker ones were culled, the remainder evolving into a good-looking and hardy equine that was to become known as the Waler, after the colony of New South Wales.

Infusions of Arab blood have since been added, as well as more Thoroughbred and Welsh Mountain Pony, and in recent times the American Quarter Horse has been used. The resulting Australian Stock Horse is an animal of exceptional quality, with good bone, hard feet and superb paces – a tough but stylish equine.

Waler

conformation attractive head, well-sloped shoulders,
strong back, powerful legs, big, clean joints
colour bay, chestnut, black, brown, grey
height 15–16 hands
uses all-rounder

Seven horses arrived in what was to become New South Wales, on Australia's eastern coast, with the First Fleet in 1788: five mares, one stallion and one colt. They were to form the basis of what was perhaps the best cavalry mount ever – although it began as a nickname for horses from New South Wales, the Waler type began to emerge and his reputation as a versatile all-rounder started to grow.

By the end of the 19th century, Australian horses were being exported to India alone at a rate of 5,000 per year, and Australia became the sole supplier of remount horses to the British and Indian armies of the subcontinent.

In the early 20th century, more Thoroughbred blood was added, as was that of draught breeds such as the Clydesdale, but this was found to be detrimental to the stamina of the Waler and Arab blood was introduced to counteract it.

The modern Waler must be of Australian breeding, which has had no imports since the 1940s. He is a versatile, all-purpose equine, possessing good conformation, a tough constitution and, in many cases, an exceptional jumping ability – in 1940, a Waler was recorded jumping a height of 2.54 m (8ft 4in).

'The Waler has an exceptional jumping ability'

Batak

conformation fine head with straight or slightly concave profile, medium length of rein, high 'goose' rump, slender legs
colour all solid colours
height up to 13 hands
uses riding, harness

With his small, elegant head, large, expressive eyes and spirited temperament, the Batak Pony of central Sumatra, Indonesia, clearly displays his Arabian influences. Sometimes referred to as the Deli Pony – after the port from which he was exported to Singapore – he is thought to have descended from horses brought to Indonesia centuries ago by Chinese-Mongolian and Arabian horse dealers.

The Batak tribes on the island were reliant on these equines, which were prized as much for their meat as for their working abilities. They were considered 'unviolable and non-alienable'. Each clan would keep three Batak Ponies, which were allowed to roam freely until they grew old, when they were sacrificed to the 'trinity of gods' that the tribes worshipped, and replaced with younger animals. They were also sometimes used to pay a bad debt – a creditor could allow his debtor to slaughter his pony and hold a public feast as repayment.

Today, the Indonesian government strives to improve existing stock by selective breeding, as well as using the Batak to upgrade other breeds. He is very much a working animal and his kind nature, docility and agility make him a superb riding pony.

Caspian

conformation neat, pretty head, long, supple neck, short-coupled, long, slender legs, strong feet
colour all solid colours
height 10–13 hands
uses riding, harness

Imagine an Arab scaled down to about 12 hands, and you have the Caspian. This beguiling little creature is most certainly a horse and not a pony, and is as ancient a breed as the 'scaled-up' model.

He is thought to date back to around 3000 BC and small equines feature in carvings and on friezes of that era. Darius the Great, ruler of Mesopotamia around 500 BC, so favoured these courageous, swift little horses that he honoured them by using their likeness on the royal seal.

However, the breed was thought to be extinct until a small number of little horses was found in the 1960s by an American called Louise Firouz, who wrote in 1968: 'We are still searching for them: diminutive... Arab-looking creatures with big bold eyes, prominent jaws and high-set tails which so distinguish their larger cousins.'

Mrs Firouz and her team discovered about 50 of these little horses along the southern coast of the Caspian Sea, 30 of them concentrated in a comparatively small area – the remainder were thought to be so scattered that they could not be pure. She took seven mares and six stallions as foundation stock to revitalize the breed.

Hokkaido

conformation plain head, carried low on a short neck, thickset body, slender legs, good feet

colour bay, brown, chestnut, roan, cremello, often with dorsal stripe, no white markings

height 13–13.2 hands

uses trail riding, packhorse, harness

All Japan's equines are thought to have descended from animals brought from the mainland of Asia at various times and by various routes, although there were certainly domesticated horses in Japan in the 6th century, and perhaps even earlier.

The Hokkaido – sometimes called Dosanko – is thought to have been brought to Hokkaido, the northernmost of the four main islands of Japan, during the Edo era (1600–1867) by fishermen from Honshu, who sailed across the Tsugaru Strait in search of herring. Their horses were used for transport, but when the fishermen went home in the autumn, they left the horses behind, to survive as best they could in a snow-bound land. When the fishermen returned the following spring, they brought new horses, which again would be left behind to fend for themselves. Only the hardiest animals survived and thrived, resulting in the abiding strength for which the Hokkaido is renowned.

Today's Hokkaido is exceptionally strong for his size and is easy-going and willing. Many ranchers still winter their horses in the mountains, which ensures the hardiness of the breed. The horses feed mainly on bamboo grass, and in spring return naturally to the ranches, because this is when the mountain bears awaken from hibernation and will prey on the Hokkaido foals.

Java

conformation large, plain head, short, thick neck, upright
shoulders, weak legs, often cow-hocked
colour all colours
height 12.2 hands
uses harness, riding

Somewhat unprepossessing in his appearance, the little Java
Pony is native to the Indonesian island of the same name.
But despite his less-than-beautiful looks, he is strong and
seemingly tireless. He is used on Java to pull *sados*, the two-
wheeled carts that serve as taxis on the island and which are
often laden with whole families and their baggage. Java is the
most densely populated island in Indonesia.

The Java is probably Chinese in origin and is thought to
date back to the 5th century BC. When Dutch settlers annexed
Indonesia and her islands in the late 16th century, the Arab
tradesmen with whom they did business brought with them
Arab and Barb horses, both of which would have had
influence on the native ponies.

Although he lacks Arabian beauty, the Java has
undoubtedly inherited his speed and endurance and is able to
thrive in the harshest of conditions. The Barb influence would
have added to the pony's desert character and extreme
toughness – and possibly to his less-than-certain temper.

At 12.2 hands high, the Java stands a little taller than most
of the other Indonesian breeds, the only larger ones being the
Batak and the Sandalwood, but he can easily carry an adult.

Kiso

conformation large head, flat withers, upright shoulders, short body, good feet
colour all colours
height 13 hands
uses draught, harness, riding

Horses from the mountainous Kiso region of central Japan were bred primarily as warhorses, some 10,000 being provided as cavalry mounts for the warrior Yoskinaka Kiso's army in the 13th century. Later, during the Edo (1600–1867) and the Meiji (1868–1903) periods, Japan was almost constantly at war, for which she needed horses, but because of the diminutive size of the Kiso, breeding pure was

discouraged and most were crossed with the bigger Western breeds. During World War II, a government edict demanded the castration of all Kiso stallions, which had a dire effect on the breed.

Were it not for the Japanese belief in keeping a sacred white horse at certain shrines, the Kiso would have died out completely, but one was found at a Shinto shrine that was kept as a holy horse and therefore not gelded. The horse, named Shinmei, and a Kiso mare named Kayama bred Dai-san Haruyama in 1951 – the last of the purebred Kiso.

The modern Kiso is a result of back-breeding among the descendants of Dai-san Haruyama and other Kiso lines. There are ranches in Japan that specialize in breeding Kisos, but there are believed to be only just over 100 left.

Misaki

conformation heavy head, short neck, compact body, slender legs
colour bay, black, chestnut
height 12.2–13 hands
uses tourism

This breed takes its name from the Cape of Toi or Toimisaki – *misaki* means 'cape' – in the Miyasaki region of Japan, a well-known and popular tourist region. Like all Japan's native breeds, the Misaki is thought to be Chinese in origin, having descended from either the plateau horses of central Asia or the Mongolian horses of the grasslands, and dates back perhaps 2,000 years. And like the Kiso and Hokkaido, the horses were religiously symbolic.

However, the first historical mention of these horses appears in 1697, when the Akizuki family of the Takanabe clan took wild horses under its protection and established a stud farm. Breeding stock was given full freedom to roam at will, being rounded up once a year to select horses to be domesticated, check the health of the remaining herd, and castrate colts and stallions that were deemed unsuitable for breeding. This same system is still used today, with the horses being corralled and then inoculated and treated for parasites or disease.

Like many of the Japanese breeds, the Misaki is no great beauty, but the remaining herd of less than 100 – the breed numbers were greatly reduced after Word War II – has been designated a national treasure and has become a focus for the tourism industry in Japan.

Sandalwood

conformation small head, short neck, long, straight back, high-set tail, thin legs
colour all colours
height 13.1 hands
uses racing, riding

The Sandalwood is named for the sweet-smelling wood that is the principal export of the islands of Sumba and Sumbawa, and it is Indonesia's quality riding pony, with little of the Mongolian characteristics found in her other breeds.

The Dutch imported Arab stallions to Sumatra, the biggest of the Indonesian islands, and selected native mares were sent to the studs, with their resulting offspring dispersed among the other islands to improve existing stock.

Indeed, the Arabian influence is clear in the Sandalwood, in his chiselled, elegant head, deep chest and girth, and good legs and feet. He has also inherited the Arab's immunity to extreme heat – the Sandalwood hardly ever breaks sweat – and his speed and grace.

Swift and agile, the Sandalwood is often used for racing, both on the islands and in Thailand, to which he is a popular export. In Indonesia itself, the pony is raced over distances of 4–5 km (2½–3 miles), ridden bareback and in the traditional bitless bridle.

In Malaysia, Sandalwoods are crossed with Thoroughbreds to produce a bigger, faster equine, also popular in other Southeast Asian countries. But his willingness and kind nature also make the purebred Sandalwood an excellent child's pony.

Sumba/Sumbawa

conformation plain head, short neck, small body,
　　strong back, strong legs
colour dun with black dorsal stripe, dark mane and tail
height 12.2 hands
uses riding, pack pony

Indonesia's 'dancing pony' is the epitome of his primitive
ancestors, with his upright mane, almost uniform dun
colouring, black dorsal stripe and zebra markings on his legs.
Like most of the Indonesian breeds, he is not the best-looking
equine, his head being comparatively large and coarse for his
small stature – he rarely stands much above 12 hands. But he
is exceptionally hardy and very strong.

The pony comes originally from the Nusa Tenggara
province, the west of which comprises two main islands,
Lombok and Sumbawa, the east some 550, the main ones
being Flores, Sumba and Timor. The native ponies take their
name from their island of origin, but are essentially one and
the same. They are extremely robust, their native land being
harsh with poor grazing, and naturally very co-operative,
lacking the primitive type's uncertain temper. Nimble and
quick, they are ridden in the traditional bitless bridle and
competed in lance contests. The ponies can easily carry a
full-grown man, a load far out of proportion to their size.

But the most prized Sumba pony is the one that dances –
bells are attached to his knees and he dances, with elegance
and lightness, to the beat of tom-tom drums.

Basuto

conformation neat head, long neck, upright shoulders, long back, short legs, hard feet
colour chestnut, bay, brown, grey
height 14.2 hands
uses riding, trekking, polo

This equine's ancestors were the Cape Horses (see page 118), sent to the South African province from Java by the Dutch East India Company in 1652, but because of bad weather they docked at St Helena and reached the Cape only in 1655. These horses were probably of Arabian and Persian descent, being quite small but tough and robust – as they would have had to be to survive the arduous journey.

The first horses are believed to have appeared in the Lesotho region around 1825, captured from the Zulu and later from the Boers – the Boer War was, ironically, to spread the fame of the Basuto further, as a docile, surefooted and amenable equine of unsurpassed stamina.

The Basuto population in Lesotho today is estimated to be around 112,000. He is a source of pride in Lesotho and is used not only as a mode of transport over the rugged topography of the region, but also by tourists for trekking, which is a source of income for several communities. In some parts of the country, he is used as a draught animal, for ploughing, planting and cultivating the fields. A natural resource of Lesotho, as yet no serious efforts have been made to exploit the Basuto commercially.

Boer (Cape Horse)

conformation straight head, often Spanish-looking, medium-length neck, good shoulder, medium-length back, slender legs

colour all colours

height 14.2–16 hands

uses military, riding, harness, all-purpose

The growth and development of the Boer Horse are parallel and inseparably connected to the history of the white settlers in South Africa.

The merchant Jan van Riebeeck, on a commission from the Dutch East India Company, anchored on the Cape of Good Hope in 1652 and established a colony there – Cape Town is known as South Africa's 'Mother City'.

The first horses arrived in 1665, imported from Java (see page 112). To avoid inbreeding, Persian Arabs were introduced and a recognizable breed of horses – known as the Cape Horse – evolved, renowned as an excellent cavalry mount. Later, because Buenos Aires, Argentina, was the closest port, substantial numbers of Andalucians were brought to the Cape – many South African horses still retain a distinct Spanish look. Thoroughbred stallions were later used to improve the breed.

The Boer, or Cape Horse, played a major role in the Great Trek of 1836, when the settlers journeyed to colonize South Africa and other horse breeds were introduced. An epidemic – possibly African Horse Sickness, still a killer today – wiped out thousands of equines, and further losses were suffered during the Boer War (1899–1902) and World War II.

Nooitgedachter

conformation fine head, sloping shoulders, short back, good joints, excellent feet
colour bay, roan – all variations
height 13.2–15 hands
uses riding, draught

Perhaps the world's rarest equine breed, the Nooitgedachter is a worthy descendant of the Basuto, refined with some Boer and Arab blood, as well as Java. It is from these oriental ancestors that the Nooitgedachter inherited his spirit, intelligence and stamina.

His good looks echo those of the Basuto, too, his fine bone structure belying his hardy constitution and generally sturdy good health. He has strong joints and excellent feet, which rarely need to be shod. He also possesses the Basuto's kind nature and affinity with and fondness for people.

In 1951, the South African Department of Agriculture purchased a small group of ponies, and a year later initiated a breeding programme at the Nooitgedachter Research Station near Ermelo in the eastern Transvaal. Because of previous inbreeding, a selective process was adopted and only one in every four foals was kept.

By 1967, eight studs were established as part of the breeding programme. In the same year, the Nooitgedacht Breeders' Society was established and in 1976 it was recognized by the South African Stud Book Association as the country's first indigenous breed of horse. Although the Nooitgedacht is bred on more than a hundred farms, he is probably still one of the rarest horse breeds worldwide.

Indian Half-Bred

conformation plain head, well-formed withers, good back, plenty of bone, hard feet
colour all colours
height 15.2 hands
uses riding, competition

India's native horse breeds – the Marwari, Kathiawari and Sindhi – are tough and robust, making them well suited to the subcontinent's harsh climate, but they are also small and lean.

The Indian Half-Bred was developed as a larger cavalry mount in the 19th century, by crossing native stock with Australian Walers to add bone and substance, and Arabs for refinement. Later, English Thoroughbred blood was added and there is now little evidence of the Arabian influence. The Thoroughbred blood was of major benefit, as Thoroughbred horses cope well with the Indian climate.

The Indian army continued to use Thoroughbred stallions on carefully selected mares and the resulting Indian Half-Bred proved a superlative cavalry mount. One stallion, called Thomas Jefferson, produced particularly good stock and was used for several years at the army stud at Babugarh and the remount depot at Sarahanapur. With the partition of the subcontinent between India and Pakistan in 1947, India kept eight English and four French Thoroughbreds, which were to form the basis of future breeding stock.

Since then, other breeds have been used, including Anglo-Arabs, Bretons and Polish horses, but the modern Indian Half-Bred remains a wiry, enduring horse well suited to his harsh environment.

Kathiawari

conformation curled ears, plain withers and shoulders, narrow body, high tail carriage, hard feet
colour all solid colours except black, but predominantly chestnut
height 14.2–15 hands
uses police, riding, polo

Like his cousin the Marwari, this noble breed is thought to have descended from oriental horses, possibly shipped to India by the Mogul emperors and crossed there with native stock. Certainly, it is widely accepted that the breed's characteristically curling ears, which are a defining trait of both the Kathiawari and the Marwari, are due to his elegant Arabian ancestors.

The most common colour is chestnut, although all solid colours occur except black. The Kathiawari is a natural pacer, as is the Marwari, and possesses a fifth gait called the *revaal*, an exceptionally smooth and comfortable gait with minimal vertical movement. The existence of this pace is thought to point to Asian influences such as Turkmenian.

Intelligent and affectionate, the Kathiawari – who takes his name from the Kathiawar region in the state of Gujerat – was highly prized by Indian princes, each royal household having its own horse, which was treated as a favoured pet. In the early 19th century, the 'Kattywar' was renowned as an excellent warhorse and was used extensively by both the British and Mahratta cavalries.

Today, his speed and agility make him an ideal mount for traditional games such as tent-pegging and polo, and he is used throughout India as a police horse.

'the Kathiawari was highly prized by Indian princes'

Marwari

conformation long, refined head, distinctive curled ears, long shoulders, short-coupled, long legs, hard feet
colour all colours including *ablaks* (piebald or skewbald)
height 14–17 hands
uses riding, High School

According to Shri Mahant Baba Balak Dasji Maharaj, a priest and renowned horse breeder, the Marwari can be traced back to 'when the ocean was churned to extract nectar for the gods... a period when horses had wings'. Or, at least, to the 12th century.

Native to the Marwar region of India, he was the horse of warriors, renowned for his iron constitution, fleet agility and courage. He has saved many a life in the desert, his distinctive curled ears that meet in the middle enabling him to hear sounds from further away than most other equine breeds, providing both horse and rider with early warning of impending danger.

He also formed a close bond with his rider. It is said that the Marwari left the battleground in one of three ways: as a victor; as a saviour, carrying his injured rider to safety; or as a spirit, having given his life for his master.

With his days on the battleground over, fewer Marwari horses were bred, but the Maharajah of Jodhpur has taken a keen interest in this elegant equine's survival and today the horse is enjoying a reversal of fortune, saved from the threat of extinction.

'he was the horse of warriors, renowned for his iron constitution, fleet agility and courage.'

National Show Horse

conformation small head, straight or concave profile,
   pronounced withers, deep shoulders, short-coupled,
   high-set tail
colour all solid colours
height 16–16.2 hands
uses showing, riding

If the Arab horse is a living work of art, when crossed with the American Saddlebred he produces a blueprint for classic equine beauty, combined with superb, athletic paces and exceptional charisma. The ideal National Show Horse has a blend of the Arab's elegance and grace, and his strength and stamina, combined with the Saddlebred's extremely long neck, high-stepping action and showring presence.

This new breed – the National Show Horse Registry was formed in 1982 – has found a niche in the American equestrian heart. Breeders were producing Arab-Saddlebred crosses for many years and had enjoyed considerable success in the showring, but it wasn't until the latter part of the 20th century that a dedicated group of horsemen and women pushed for its recognition and promotion. In 1984, the new organization held its first national championships, paying out more than $100,000 in prize money.

Today, the National Show Horse goes from strength to strength and the breed's registry has established specific rules for breeding America's most successful equine 'peacock' – all registered horses must contain a minimum of 25 per cent and a maximum of 99 per cent Arabian blood.

'a blueprint for classic equine beauty'

Appaloosa

conformation visible sclera (white ring around iris), mottled skin, sparse mane and tail, strong back, striped feet
colour 13 base coat colours, seven coat patterns
height 14.2–15.2 hands
uses riding, rodeo, ranching

Spotted horses have been depicted in Chinese and Asian art for centuries, yet the first equines to arrive in the New World were brought by the Spanish conquistadors in the 16th century and then acquired by the Plains Indians – most notably the Nez Perce, renowned for their breeding skills and horsemanship. However, there is a theory that the Nez Perce and other Pacific northwest tribes may have migrated across a land bridge that existed between the Asian and North American continents, shortly after the last glaciers on the North American continent began to recede. If this is true, then perhaps the Nez Perce and the Appaloosa horse were linked for much longer.

Whatever the true story, the Nez Perce were a noble people and justifiably proud of their distinctive horses, which they guarded fiercely. They did not, however, coin the breed's name – it is thought to come from either the Palouse River, which flows through eastern Washington and north Idaho, or the tribe named for it. White settlers called the spotted mount of the tribe 'a Palouse horse', which was soon to become Appalousey – the name Appaloosa was officially adopted in 1938, when the society was formed. In March 1975, Cecil Adrus, Governor of Idaho, named the Appaloosa as the official state horse – a deserving honour.

Azteca

conformation lean head, straight or slightly convex profile, arched neck, deep chest, strong back, good feet
colour all solid colours
height 14.2–15.3 hands
uses riding, bullfighting, competition

Mexico's 'national breed' may be in its infancy, but it is a supreme equine success story. Before its development, Mexico had no indigenous horse breed, her equines being Spanish or Portuguese in origin.

The Mexicans had long been admirers of the Spanish horse, and the Andalucian was chosen as the foundation stock for the new national breed, crossed with American Quarter Horses and Criollos. The aim was to produce a horse with speed, agility, endurance and power. It was also to be good-looking, trainable, easy-going and courageous, as well as having spirit and heart.

And they succeeded. The first Azteca stallion, called Casarejo, was born in Texcoco: he was by the Spanish stallion Ocultado, out of the Quarter Horse mare Americana. The modern Azteca may have minimum 37.5 per cent, maximum 62.5 per cent Andalucian or Quarter Horse blood, with not more than 25 per cent Criollo.

He is a superb all-round competition horse – an elegant animal, ideal for performance or pleasure riding, athletic enough for the *charro* (Mexican rodeo) and brave enough for the bullring. He has superb paces and a good athletic jump, and his physical excellence is only surpassed by his happy and obedient temperament.

Buckskin

conformation attractive head, medium-length neck, strong
   back, good legs, hard feet
colour buckskin, dun, red dun, brindle dun, grulla/grullo,
   white markings permitted
height 15–16.3 hands
uses all-rounder

Famed for being 'as tough as wet leather', never let it be
said that the Buckskin is merely a colour. These horses
have long been noted for their superior qualities – they are
widely deemed to have more stamina, harder feet and better
bone and to be generally hardier than all other horses.
A Buckskin that has either weak or faulty legs is indeed
a rarity.

The breed is thought to have inherited its distinctive
colour from the little Sorraia – like all the horses of the
Americas, the Buckskin is Spanish in origin – and the
International Buckskin Horse Association recognizes five
different colourways.

The true buckskin colouring is the shade of tanned
deerhide, varying from yellow to dark gold, with black or
dark brown points. The dun is duller than the true buckskin
and may include dorsal, shoulder and leg stripes.
Grulla/grullo is an intense colour ranging through mouse,
blue, dove and slate, with dark brown or black points and the
'primitive' striping. Red dun ranges from peach through
copper to rich red and must have a dominant dorsal stripe to
be eligible. Brindle dun is found in the horses of the
Netherlands as well as the Buckskin, and is thought to be an
ancient colour.

*'The breed is thought
to have inherited its
distinctive colour from
the little Sorraia.'*

Choctaw

conformation neat head, straight or convex profile, short
    neck, narrow chest, medium-length back, excellent feet
colour all colours
height 13.2–14.2 hands
uses riding, trekking, harness

America's Mustang is well known – her 'Spanish Mustang', the Choctaw, less so. Brought to the Americas from Spain, some horses escaped or were let loose and roamed free. They were captured by the Native Americans, whose lives they were to transform, giving them far more freedom. In return, the tribes revered and cherished their tough little horses.

The Cherokee and Choctaw tribes in particular benefited from becoming horse owners. The latter were not great buffalo hunters and they used the horse as an agricultural animal, working the land in the centre of what is now Mississippi, and as a means of transport.

This tough, attractive and hardy little equine became known as the Choctaw Pony. To the indigenous tribesmen who prized him, he came to represent wealth, prestige, glory and honour.

By the 19th century, many of the Choctaw people had been forced to leave their homeland, and many others left of their own accord, heading for the 'promised land', which is now known as Oklahoma. As the original tribes started to die out in the 1970s, it looked as if their little horse would die with them, but the Choctaw has been saved from extinction and several small pure herds are being preserved for their size, stamina and disposition.

Criollo

conformation short, broad head, often convex profile, muscular neck, short, deep body, strong legs
colour predominantly dun, also chestnut, bay, grey, roan, black
height 14–15 hands
uses riding, polo, stock work

Argentina's Criollo – or Creole – is the king of the Pampas, the grassland around the delta of the Rio de la Plata. The horses were originally feral, either abandoned or escaped from conquistador stock, for which the natural selection process was particularly harsh. These herds were mixed with horses brought by travellers from Brazil, Uruguay and Chile. Portuguese and Dutch blood was later introduced via Brazil.

With the British arrival in Argentina came the introduction of Thoroughbred blood to lighten and refine existing stock, and later, with the French, Percheron to add substance and make a heavier draught type. The new blood of both proved detrimental to the Criollo, and in 1917 the Sociedad Rural de Argentina was established to preserve the breed.

A herd of 200 mares, which had been kept by the Native American people of the south, became the foundation for the rehabilitation of the old breed, which is revered for its endurance and stamina.

In 1925–28, Aimé Tschiffely rode from Buenos Aires to Washington DC on two Criollo geldings in order to prove the hardiness and stamina of the breed – both survived the trip and lived to an old age back in their homeland.

Cremello

conformation varies
colour white to rich cream or pale gold, blue or amber eyes
height varies
uses riding, harness, pleasure riding, showing

American White or Cremello horses have been popular for some years – traditionally, white horses were considered the most beautiful and highly desirable, ridden by royalty and thought to have magical powers. But their light colouring was also thought to be a sign of weakness, which is just as mythical. It is often said a good horse is never a bad colour…

These pale horses were championed in America by Caleb and Hudson Thompson, and Caleb's wife, Ruth, founded the Albino Registry in Nebraska in 1937. Their foundation stallion was an Arab-Morgan cross called Old King and the Thompsons used him on Morgan mares to create a breed of white or cream horses. The Albino Registry was later opened to any horse – not just Old King stock – that was white or cream.

The American Creme Horse Registry was opened in 1980, and although all breeds may be registered, the colour has to conform to registry standards. The Cremello must have pink skin, with no mottling or spots. His eyes can be any colour, but most commonly will be pale blue or a very pale amber. His coat may vary from off-white to a fairly rich cream, but must be lighter than palomino. White markings such as blazes, stars and socks are permitted.

Contrary to popular belief, Cremellos are no more prone to deafness or blindness than any other breed.

Falabella

conformation neat head, in proportion to body, medium-
length neck and back, legs in proportion
colour all colours
height 76–82.5 cm (30–32½ in)
uses pet, showing, harness

It is said that there is no place in the world where a Falabella has not trodden, and indeed this beguiling little horse – and he is a miniature horse, not a pony – is universally popular. His origins lie in Argentina and undoubtedly date back to the Andalucian horses introduced by the Spanish.

Either escaped or abandoned, these horses roamed the Pampas, a harsh and arid environment with merciless sun, cold southwestern winds and violent storms. The horses often travelled great distances to find food and water, and hence only the toughest survived. These factors, along with continual inbreeding, must surely have resulted in some genetic mutations.

The Falabella family of Buenos Aires first saw a herd of tiny, but perfect, horses with the Mapuche Indians in the mid-19th century. Having acquired some, they then set out to produce a uniform breed of horse standing no higher than 1 m (40 in) – later, they refined the breed using small Thoroughbreds, Welsh ponies, Shetlands and Criollos, and dropped the height limit to 76 cm (30 in).

The modern Falabella is conformationally sound, stands a maximum of 82.5 cm (32½ in) and is perfectly proportioned. Gregarious in the field and naturally hardy, his charming temperament makes him an ideal family pet.

Florida Cracker

conformation refined, intelligent head, narrow, well-defined neck, short, strong back, sloping croup, low-set tail
colour all colours
height 13–15.2 hands
uses riding, ranching, pleasure riding

Cowboys in Florida were nicknamed 'crackers' because of the sound their whips made cracking in the air, and their agile little horses became known by the same name. Spanish in origin, the Florida Cracker was essential to the cattle industry in that state, which began almost 500 years ago and flourishes today. Over the years, Cracker horses have been known by a variety of names, among them Chickasaw Pony, Seminole Pony, March Tackie, Prairie Pony, Florida Horse, Florida Cow Pony and Grass Gut. Because of the comparative isolation of Florida, and her constant trade with Cuba, the Spanish bloodlines were continually refreshed.

Following the Great Depression of the 1930s, cattle were moved into Florida from the Dust Bowl of the Mid-West, bringing with them a parasite called screw worm. This changed ranching practices – instead of being driven by the cowboys, the cattle now had to be roped so they could be treated for the worm. The Florida Cracker fell from favour, to be replaced by the bigger, stronger Quarter Horse.

The breed has been saved, however, and its fans say the best way to tell a Florida Cracker horse is to ride one – its easy, ground-covering gaits are rarely found in other breeds.

Galiceno

conformation neat head on slender neck, upright shoulders, narrow, compact body, short back, slim legs
colour all solid colours
height 12–14 hands
uses riding, harness

When Hernando Cortés landed in Mexico from Cuba in 1519, he brought with him 16 horses, among them a small, lighter framed equine to use in the mines, and to carry the dead and wounded from the battlefield.

Courageous, intelligent and strong, these little horses came from the Galicia region of Spain and were believed to be crosses between Andalucian stallions and wild Sorraia and Garrano ponies. Spanish shepherds used Andalucians for herding and would release them at night, when they would be free to mate with the mountain ponies, with wandering Sorraia stallions adding to the mix.

In Mexico, they became known as Galicenos and were attractive creatures possessing the Spanish gaits and proud bearing of their Andalucian ancestors. They were greatly prized by the native people on the coastal regions of Mexico and remain popular today.

Not all are naturally gaited, depending on their heritage, but because most are it was written into the breed standard set up in the 1950s, when a number of Galicenos were captured in Mexico.

Although small, they have great presence and enough strength to carry an adult, while their docile and gentle nature makes them excellent children's ponies.

Miniature

conformation neat head, with broad forehead, in proportion with neck, sloping shoulders, short back, straight legs
colour all colours
height maximum 86.3 cm (34 in)
uses pet, showing, harness

He is billed as 'the horse for everyone', a perfectly scaled-down model of a conformationally sound equine. The first true miniature horses – as opposed to ponies, such as the Shetland – were bred in Europe as pampered pets of the nobility, although the less lucky, or less attractive, ones were worked in coalmines. There are records and pictures of miniature horses dating as far back as the 18th century.

It is possible they first found favour in America during the Gold Rush that began in 1848, being hooked up to carts that they were small enough to pull through the mines – miniatures can pull up to ten times their own weight and possess great stamina. Today, while still popular as pets and companions, they are found in all sorts of competition and harness classes.

The miniature ideal is of a perfectly formed small horse, with mares showing femininity and refinement, and stallions muscularity and boldness. They must be sound, well balanced and possess the correct conformation characteristics required of most breeds. The general impression should be one of symmetry, strength, agility and alertness.

They are also gentle, affectionate and eager to please – big fun in a small package.

'miniatures can pull up to ten times their own weight and possess great stamina'

Tennessee Walking Horse

conformation pretty head, long shoulders, short-coupled,
  longer bottomline than topline, flowing mane and tail
colour all colours
height 14.3–17 hands
uses showing, pleasure riding, trail riding

This is the first American breed to bear the name of a state, and Tennesseans are justly proud of their home-grown horse. A gaited breed, he is a composite of the Narragansett Pacer, Standardbred, Morgan and Thoroughbred, combining the beauty and fire of all those breeds.

The Tennessee Walker possesses a natural, inherited gait, the running walk, which is ideal for covering the state's rocky terrain in comfort and at speed. This gait cannot be taught, and is the Tennessee breed's most cherished quality. He also has two other gaits, the 'flat-foot walk', which is slow but powerful and even, and the 'rocking-chair gait', a particularly springy, rhythmic, rolling canter. At the running walk, he can maintain a speed of 16–32 kmph (10–20 mph). As the speed is increased, the horse oversteps the front track with the back by a distance of 15–45 cm (6–18 in). The more 'stride' the horse has, the better 'walker' he is considered to be.

He may also perform the rack, stepping pace, fox trot and single-foot, although these are not desirable in the showring.

Tennessee Walkers were developed for riding and driving, as well as farm work. They were popular with plantation owners, who called them Plantation Walkers and would ride them for long distances across their vast properties, their steady paces easy on their rider. Country doctors favoured the breed, too, because they spent many hours in the saddle, as did travelling preachers. The Tennessee Walker could stride effortlessly over the hills and valleys of his home state, maintaining his even and steady pace for long distances.

In 1886, a black colt with a white blaze was born, the result of a mating between a stallion called Allendorf, from the Hambletonian trotting family, and Maggie Marshall, a Morgan mare. The colt was called Black Allen, and was to become the Tennessee Walking Horse Breeders' Association's foundation sire. Crossed with a pacer, he produced the first recognized Tennessee Walker.

With its association established in 1935, the Tennessee Walking Horse is one of the fastest-growing equine breeds, with more than 300,000 registered. Handsome and showy, he is also affectionate, kind and intelligent.

He excels in the showring, performing his unique gaits with verve and vigour. It is little wonder that this equine superstar is called the world's greatest show horse – he possesses beauty, poise and dignity.

'the world's greatest show horse – he possesses beauty, poise and dignity'

Mangalarga Marchador

conformation long head, short back, strong hindquarters, long legs, low-set tail
colour bay, chestnut, roan, grey
height 14–16 hands
uses riding, harness, ranching

This horse was originally called Sublime, a name that encompasses all that is great about Brazil's national horse breed. Sublime was a Spanish stallion, thought to be an Alter-Real, that was presented in 1812 to Gabriel Francisco Junqueira, Baron of Aldenas and owner of the Hacienda Campo Alegre, by Prince Pedro I, later to become emperor of Brazil. The baron bred Sublime to mares of Spanish Jennet and North African Barb blood, and the resulting progeny were known as Sublime horses.

The stallion passed on his good looks and his gait, a smooth running walk that was extremely comfortable, known as the *marcha*. Some of his offspring were purchased from Campo Alegre by the Hacienda Mangalarga, which continued selective breeding, and the horses became known as the Mangalarga Marchador.

Some experimentation with American Saddlebred, Thoroughbred and Arabian blood led to a separate registry, for Mangalarga Paulista Horses, in 1934. But the original Mangalarga breed has been kept remarkably pure, based on the original foundation lines from Campo Alegre – genetic studies were conducted that show very little or no outside influences – to produce horses that are surefooted, graceful and of excellent temperament.

The first breed association was established in 1949 and the Mangalarga's gaits remain his hallmark. He has three distinctive gaits: the *marcha picada*, a lateral gait, ranging from a swift running walk to a pace similar to the Icelandic flying *tölt*; the *marcha batida*, a diagonal gait similar to the foxtrot or Peruvian *troche*; and the 'center march', much like the classic running walk of the Tennessee Walking Horses of the 1930s–40s.

But he is not just about his paces. The Mangalarga is a horse of great beauty and impressive presence, combined with a docile nature and kind temperament. He is also highly intelligent and possesses considerable stamina, which makes him popular in the hunting field.

To prove the endurance of the breed, in 1994 two Brazilians completed a trail ride of 13, 910 km (8,694 miles) on Mangalarga Marchador horses. They rode all day and rested at night, and the trip took them one and a half years – on the same horses. The remarkable feat was recorded in the *Guinness Book of Records*.

Today, the breed is rigorously performance tested to preserve and protect its finer characteristics, and continues to excel in many spheres. From his beginnings almost 200 years ago, the Mangalarga Marchador remains sublime.

'horses that are surefooted, graceful and of excellent temperament'

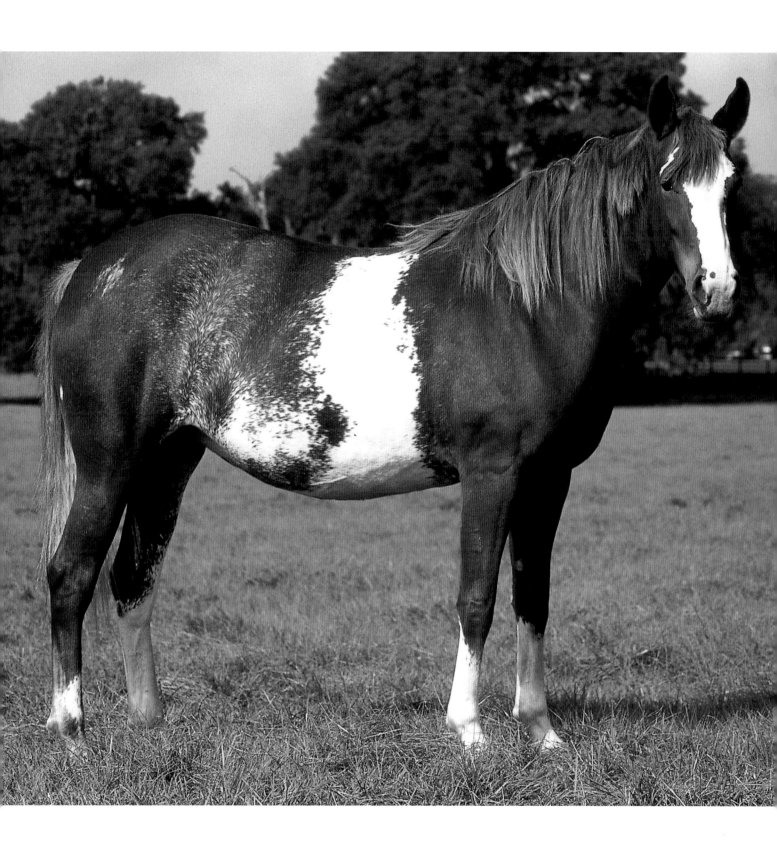

Missouri Fox Trotter

conformation neat, clean head, sloping shoulders, short, strong back, well-muscled legs, strong feet
colour most colours
height 14–16 hands
uses riding, showing, pleasure riding

Missouri was recognized as a state in 1821, and her horse breed was developed in the Ozark Mountains during the 19th century by settlers who needed strong, durable equines that could cover long distances at a comfortable pace. These settlers came from Kentucky, Tennessee and Virginia, and brought with them their own stock, mostly Morgans and Arabs. Later, Saddlebred, Standardbred and Tennessee Walking Horse blood were added.

With the introduction of gaited breeds, the Ozark Hill Horse was developed and encouraged, his smooth, swinging 'fox trot' proving the most comfortable and most practical for work in the mountains. The fox trot is a diagonal gait, with the horse appearing to walk with his forelegs while trotting with his hindlegs, the hind feet overtracking (stepping beyond the tracks of) the front. Because of this sliding action, the Fox Trotter's unique gait is incredibly comfortable, as well as being surefooted. The Missouri Fox Trotter also possesses great stamina, being able to keep up a steady speed of 8–13 kmph (5–8 mph).

Gentle and kind, the Missouri Fox Trotter is known as the common man's pleasure horse, and is in great demand – about 52,000 are registered throughout the United States, Canada and Europe.

Morab

conformation intelligent, attractive head, sloping shoulders,
 medium-length back, long croup, powerful hindquarters
colour bay, black, roan, grey, chestnut
height 14.3–16.1 hands
uses competition, endurance, showing

Take the best characteristics of two of the most beautiful and
charismatic horse breeds – the Arab and the Morgan – and
combine them to create the Morab, a gem of equine heritage.

The roots of the Morab date back to the 19th century,
when breeders were trying to perfect an all-round working
horse. Many Arab crosses were experimented with, but the
combination of Morgan and Arabian blood proved enduring.

Renowned publisher William Randolph Hearst, who bred
both Arabs and, to a lesser extent, Morgans, coined the name
Morab for the progeny of his two Arab stallions, Ksar and
Ghazi, which he crossed with Morgan mares. On his death in
1951, the breed – still in its infancy – was almost lost, although
some breeders continued to develop and evolve the Morab.

Among these was Martha Doyle Fuller, who produced
Morabs for the show circuit. Her daughter, Irene Miller,
started the first Morab registry in 1973, and the breed grew
in stature and reputation until her death in 1980. Mrs Miller
was nicknamed Mrs Morab, and through her endeavour and
determination the breed survived and thrived. The Purebred
Morab Horse Association continues her hard work today,
producing a horse that is both good-looking and versatile.

Morgan

conformation slightly concave profile, thick neck, deep
   chest, well-formed withers, strong legs
colour predominantly black, bay, brown, chestnut
height 14.2–15.2 hands
uses riding, competition, harness

One stallion, a little bay called Figure, was to found a whole breed that is as popular and enduring today as when it began in the 1790s. Figure was given to a school teacher named Justin Morgan from Randolph, Vermont, in partial payment of a debt. The little horse stood only just over 14 hands and, perhaps because of this, his new owner was unable to find a buyer for him.

Figure was of unknown breeding, although thought to be English in lineage – some speculate he was a Thoroughbred, others believe he was a Welsh Cob or perhaps a mixture of both. Whichever, and despite his short stature, he was an exceptionally good-looking horse, with a fine, intelligent head; large, expressive eyes; neat ears; well-muscled neck and shoulder; and good, clean legs.

Figure was also easy-going and strong, and people began to talk about the exploits of 'the Justin Morgan horse'. He was able to pull a log no draught horse could move; he had the beauty, spirit and manners to carry President James Monroe on a muster-day parade ground; and he outran the most successful racehorse central Vermont had ever known – until then. So popular was he, that even those who had lost bets on him would drink to his honour, toasting 'the little Morgan'.

The horse was soon to become known as Justin Morgan, after his owner, as was the custom of the day. He also proved prepotent, passing on his looks and abilities to his offspring. He lived to the age of 32, having served countless mares during his lifetime. Three of his best known sons – Sherman, Bulrush and Woodbury – were to continue the breed, and all modern Morgans can be traced back to these three sires.

As America grew, so did the Morgan breed and its reputation. Men answered the call of the Gold Rush on the backs of Morgan horses. The Vermont Cavalry rode into the Civil War on Morgans – the Union's General Sheridan on Rienzi, the Confederate's Stonewall Jackson on Little Sorrel.

And the only survivor in the Battle of Little Big Horn was Captain Myles Keogh's Morgan-bred horse Comanche.

Today's Morgan still shows the glory of his lineage, and is highly valued for the beauty, intelligence and willing charm of that one stallion. His proud carriage, soundness and athleticism shine through whether he is ridden in a Western or traditional English saddle, and he is a calm and sensible ride.

He is America's first light horse breed, and on his back rest the fortunes and heritage of that great and mighty nation.

Paint

conformation refined head and neck, short-coupled, plenty of bone, good legs
colour tobiano, overo, tovero
height varies
uses pleasure riding, showing, ranching, racing, rodeo, trail riding

They were revered by the Native Americans as possessing magical powers, but to the cowboys these colourful creatures of the Great Plains represented strong, willing and reliable working partners.

The two-toned horses were descendants of the Spanish stock; captured and gentled, they were to prove willing and hardy, ideal for herding buffalo and cattle. Decorated by Mother Nature, they were highly prized although they were later refined, but retained their exotic colouring. Each generation passed its unique coat patterns and markings down to the next. The aim was to produce a quality stock type, with the striking coat patterns of tobiano and overo.

The tobiano's head is of a solid colour, occasionally with a blaze, star, stripe or snip. His neck and chest will be spotted, with dark colour on one or both flanks. His legs will usually have white socks and his tail may be two-toned.

The overo is predominantly either dark or white, but the white will not cross his back between his withers and his tail, his markings will be irregular, and one or more legs will be dark. He may also have a 'bald' (white) face – hence skewbald and piebald. A third pattern, tovero, combines both tobiano and overo markings.

The American Paint Horse Association was formed in 1962 – today, there are about 250,000 registrations.

Palomino

conformation varies
colour pale to dark gold, white mane and tail
height varies
uses riding, ranching, rodeo, showing

Only in the United States is the Palomino recognized as a breed, rather than a colour. He should be the colour of a newly-minted 14-carat gold coin, with a coat that glows like the setting sun, dark skin and eyes, and a mane and tail of the purest white.

The origins of the Palomino are unknown, although because the colour is a dilution of a basic gene, it is probably as old as the horse himself. Certainly, the gold colour existed in China, and is found throughout history – horses of a pale golden hue are featured in Sandro Botticelli's work *The Adoration of the Magi*, painted around 1475. Palominos were probably brought to the Americas from Spain, where the colouring found favour with Queen Isabella (1451–1504) – the gold colour is still sometimes called isabella.

The Palomino Horse Breeders of America Inc. was formed in the 1930s, with three basic divisions: the stock type, predominantly represented by Quarter Horses; the Golden American Saddlebred, typically represented by Saddlebreds; and the pleasure type, exemplified by Morgan, part-bred Arabians and Tennessee Walking Horses. The palomino colour is not permitted in Thoroughbreds and Arabs. These golden horses were an almost instant success in the Americas and their popularity, like their colour, remains undimmed.

'He is the colour of a newly minted gold coin, with a coat that glows like the setting sun'

Paso Fino

conformation well-shaped head with straight or slightly
   convex profile, sloping shoulders, well-rounded rump,
   strong legs
colour all solid colours
height 13–15 hands
uses riding, showing

He is called *los caballos la Paso Fino* – the horse with the fine
walk. The Paso Fino reflects his Spanish heritage through
his proud carriage, grace and elegance. A mixture of
Andalucian, Barb and Spanish Jennet blood produced his
early forebears, who were probably introduced by the
conquistadors to the New World, where the glory of the horse
grew with the Americas. The Paso Fino was saved from
further dilution by the Puerto Ricans, who regarded him as
their national horse and guarded his breeding jealously.
It was not until after World War II that the breed was
rediscovered by American soldiers stationed in the
South Americas.

Like his close cousin, the Peruvian Paso, the Paso Fino
is one of the few five-gaited breeds that perform a lateral –
rather than diagonal – pace. The sequence of the hooves is:
right hind, right fore, left hind, left fore, with the hind foot
touching the ground a fraction of a second before the front
foot. This four-beat gait virtually eliminates the jarring effect
of a true pace.

As well as giving a luxurious ride, the Paso Fino has great
stamina and can keep up a steady pace of about 17.5 kmph
(11 mph), making him a highly desirable equine partner.
Regal and elegant, stylish and proud, his commanding
presence makes him a natural showman.

Pinto

conformation varies
colour tobiano, overo
height varies
uses varies

Quality with colour personifies the Pinto, which differs from the Paint in that technically he is a colourway, rather than a breed. Valued by the Native Americans as a warhorse – his broken coat provided excellent camouflage – and immortalized in story, verse and song, the Pinto's fortunes are inexorably tied to those of the New World.

He was originally brought from Europe by the conquistadors, who imported North African and Spanish stock – but the striking markings appear in ancient art throughout the Middle East, and evidence of broken coated equines among the wild horses of the Russian steppes suggests that the introduction of these colourings to European horses goes back much further.

Like the Paint, Pinto horses have two different colourways – tobiano and overo – but the Pinto Horse Association (PtHA) allows for the registration of miniature horses, ponies and horses derived from other breed crosses, such as Arab, Morgan, Saddlebred and Tennessee Walking Horse. In addition, the PtHA also allows solid-coloured animals with a documented and registered Pinto sire or dam into its breeding stock section.

Registered animals are divided into stock, hunter, pleasure and saddle types, ensuring the enduring success of the Pinto horse.

'His striking markings appear in ancient art throughout the Middle East'

Peruvian Paso

conformation straight or concave profile, crested neck, short back, strong hindquarters, angled hocks
colour all solid colours
height 14–15.3 hands
uses riding, harness, pleasure riding, showing

Four hundred years of selective breeding have resulted in an equine *tour de force*, but the Peruvian Paso's spectacular gaits are entirely natural, rather than taught. Up to the beginning of the 17th century, almost all horses were naturally gaited – possessing the smooth, running walk – and trotters, called 'boneshakers', were comparatively rare.

What followed was one of the most extraordinary developments ever seen in the horse. The world was changing considerably during that century: a network of roads was created and people travelled more by horse-drawn carriage than on horseback – and a trotting horse was more suited to pulling a vehicle than a gaited horse. At the same time, vast tracts of land were given over to raising cattle, where a trotting horse, again, had the advantage. Horseracing, too, became increasingly popular, another discipline at which a gaited horse did not excel. At the beginning of the 17th century it was unusual to find a horse that trotted – by its end, it was rare to find one that did not.

The Peruvian Paso, meanwhile, continued to be esteemed by the Peruvian people. Their horse was descended from Spanish stock, which combined Barb, Friesian, Jennet and Andalucian blood. In Peru, these horses were kept pure, with no outside blood, ensuring the breed retained its natural inherited gait. And of all the gaited horses, he is said to be the only one who can be guaranteed to pass his gait to 100 per cent of his offspring.

The natural gait of the Paso is known as *paso llano*, a broken gait consisting of a harmonic and rhythmic tapping in which he makes a gentle and pleasing alternating movement, while his centre of gravity remains almost immobile. It is supremely comfortable for the rider as well as ground-covering. But he also possesses a unique pace called *termino*, a graceful, flowing movement in which the forelegs are rolled from the shoulder towards the outside as the horse strides forwards, in a similar way to the arm motion of a swimmer in front crawl.

The Peruvians have a policy of not breeding from any horse, no matter how fine, that is of uncertain temperament. But this is not to say the Paso lacks spirit: a valued trait is *brio*, an arrogance and exuberance inherent in his every move, as well as stamina and willingness, all of which make him a joy to watch as well as to ride.

*'his inherent
exuberance makes
him a joy to watch
as well as to ride'*

Polo Pony

conformation lean, refined head, good length of rein,
    medium-length back, long, lean legs, sound feet
colour all solid colours
height 15–15.3 hands
uses polo

A fast, tough game, polo demands the speed of the Thoroughbred, the intelligence of the Arab and the agility of the Quarter Horse. Put those together and you get the Polo Pony, not a breed as such, but a recognized – and highly desirable – type combining the best qualities of equine excellence. Top Polo Ponies are reputed to change hands for small fortunes.

When the British first discovered the game of polo in what was then Persia, the ponies used for playing were only about 12.2 hands, which was raised to a limit of 14 hands in 1876 – the upper height limit was abolished in 1919. Although Polo Ponies now are usually about 15 hands, and are more correctly small horses, they are always referred to as ponies.

A Thoroughbred stallion called Rosewater is credited with being the English foundation sire; American ponies are usually Thoroughbred crossed with Quarter Horses for their agility and ability to 'turn on a dime'. But since the 1930s, the best Polo Ponies have come from Argentina, where the Thoroughbred is crossed with tough little native Criollos. Every Polo Pony possesses the traits that any athlete, human or equine, needs: he has heart and he yearns to be the best.

Pony of the Americas

conformation refined head with dished profile,
  good shoulders, deep chest, short back, rounded
  body, short legs
colour Appaloosa colours and patterns
height 11.2–13.2 hands
uses riding, equitation, trail riding, endurance, showing

This breed owes its existence to one colt – the result of a mating between a Shetland and an Arab-Appaloosa – called Black Hand. The colt belonged to lawyer Les Boomhower, who had been offered his dam. When the colt was born, his owner was intrigued by his spotted coat, which also showed a distinctive black 'hand' on his hindquarters.

Boomhower purchased Black Hand, and a new registry – the Pony of the Americas Club – was established in 1954. The breed standards were stringent. The pony must be no smaller than 11 hands, and no higher than 13 hands. His head must be refined, with a distinctly dished profile, and his body well muscled like that of a Quarter Horse. He must be spotted like an Appaloosa, and his markings must be visible from 12 m (40 ft) away. Perhaps even more important was his temperament – the POA is a child's pony and must be gentle and kind, easy to train and handle, but with presence and sparkle for the showring.

From Black Hand, the first POA, the club now has well over 40,000 registrations. And the pony has grown in stature, too – the height range is now 11.2–13.2 hands.

Quarter Horse

conformation short head, muscular neck, short-coupled
body, powerful hindquarters, fine legs
colour all solid colours
height 14–15.3 hands
uses racing, riding, rodeo, ranching

Contrary to popular belief, the 'Quarter' in this horse's name does not indicate the amount of Thoroughbred blood, although the latter was to play a major role in his development. America's first horse breed can sprint like lightning over a distance of a quarter of a mile (0.4 km) – he was thus known as a 'quarter-miler' or Quarter Horse.

It is thought that the basis of the Quarter Horse was Chickasaw ponies obtained from Native Americans. These were of Spanish origin, probably containing Arab, Turk and Barb blood as well as Andalucian. They were blocky little creatures that, when crossed with Thoroughbreds, produced small, muscular horses with explosive speed. Their colonial owners enjoyed competing them in short sprint races and the little Quarter Horses came into their own, easily outpacing their bigger cousins.

These races were popular in the 17th century, with the fastest sprinters being called Celebrated American Running Horses. The first races were held at Enrico County, Virginia, with two horses pitted against each other running down village streets, along country lanes and over flat pasture. With large prizes on offer and extensive heavy betting, disagreements and skirmishes were a common occurrence. It is said that some of the grander plantations changed ownership on the outcome of these one-on-one matches.

With the growth in popularity of the English Thoroughbred in the 19th century, oval racetracks were built and distance racing began to be preferred over the sprints. To a degree, the chunky Quarter Horse fell out of favour.

Luckily, racing was not his only speciality. He made an excellent stock horse, quick to start, easy to stop and able to turn on the proverbial dime. He also possessed an innate 'cow sense', a trait prized perhaps above all others. As the pioneers moved westwards in the 19th century, they took the Quarter Horse with them.

Inevitably, the breed was diluted – fast horses whose offspring proved good cow ponies were crossed with the existing mares. Traditionally, horses were named after their owners, and the names changed when the horse was sold on, making it almost impossible to keep track of bloodlines.

However, a horse foaled in 1843 called Steel Dust was to have a lasting effect on the breed. His progeny were originally called Steel Dust Horses, but when the American Quarter Horse Association was founded in 1940, the new name was officially adopted. Today, there are more than three million Quarter Horses registered.

'quick to start,
easy to stop and able
to turn on the
proverbial dime'

Racking (Single-foot) Horse

conformation elegant head, long, graceful neck,
    sloping shoulders, full flanks, fine legs
colour all colours, including spots and paints
height 15.2 hands
uses showing, pleasure riding, harness

Renowned for his beauty, stamina and docile temperament, the Racking Horse grew with America's great plantations before the Civil War. Plantation owners discovered that this noble equine could carry them around their vast estates in comfort, for hours, at a smooth, natural gait.

The 'rack' is a fast, even gait in which each foot meets the ground separately at equal intervals – it is often called a 'single-foot', because only one foot strikes the ground at a time. The head remains still, the shoulders and quarters are very active, and the horse appears to jump from one foot to another as he moves.

The Racking Horse's origins are undoubtedly with the Tennessee Walking Horse, but he was recognized as a separate breed and the registry established – largely thanks to the efforts of Alabama businessman Joe D. Bright – in 1971. The influences of the founding stock are still apparent, although the 'rack' has more collection than the Tennessee breed's distinctive running walk.

The Racking Horse is called the most versatile breed, from showring to work field, and since the 1970s he has become increasingly popular. He combines his supremely comfortable 'single-foot' gait with great grace and elegance and a gentle, affectionate disposition.

Rocky Mountain Horse®

conformation attractive head, medium length of rein, wide chest, strong back, good legs and feet
colour all solid colours, no white above knee or hock
height 14.2–16 hands
uses pleasure riding, trail riding, endurance, competition

Legend has it that in the 1890s a young horse appeared in eastern Kentucky, in the foothills of the Appalachians. A rich chocolate-brown with flaxen mane and tail, his breeding and provenance are unknown. He was to found a line of gentle, medium-sized horses with a natural, ambling, four-beat gait that was extremely comfortable. He was to give rise to a line of horses that have been treasured ever since.

In the early to mid-20th century, Sam Tuttle of Spout Springs, Kentucky, organized rides through the Natural Bridge State Park, and found these horses the perfect mounts for everyone, young or old, no matter what their riding ability. He nurtured and promoted the breed, using a stallion called Old Tobe, who continued to breed well into his thirties, to perpetuate the Rocky Mountain Horse®.

As well as easy gaits, these horses were surefooted and robust. They were the mounts of choice for postmen, doctors and travelling preachers; they were used to plough fields, herd cattle and pull the cart to church on Sundays.

All the horses from the Old Tobe line retained their striking colour, sweet nature and smooth gait – it is said his offspring followed in his perfectly timed hoofbeats.

Saddlebred

conformation small head, arched neck, short, strong body, slim, clean legs, high tail carriage
colour most solid colours
height 15–17 hands
uses riding, showing

The ancestors of America's favourite riding horse were Irish Hobbies and Galloways, shipped to the United States in the 17th century. They were hardy little horses and thrived in their new environment, their offspring becoming known as Narragansett Pacers after the Narragansett Bay area of Rhode Island.

But the Pacers' fame and popularity grew – they were natural pacers, performing the lateral four-beat gait with all four legs moving independently that is also known as the 'rack' – and they were soon being bred widely across the eastern seaboard.

The Narragansett Pacer is now extinct, although the Paso Fino is probably very similar. The first Thoroughbreds arrived in America in the 16th century and, when crossed with Narragansett Pacers, produced a horse with the size and beauty of the former, plus the easy gait and calm willingness of the latter. By 1776, there was a recognized breed of 'American Horse'.

The American cavalry won their battle with the British at Kings Mountain in South Carolina on his back, and he was later to carry his masters through the Cumberland Gap and into what is now Kentucky. There was some outcrossing of the American Horse to Thoroughbreds, Standardbreds and Morgans, but he retained his beauty and presence, and his ability to rack.

Kentucky is still renowned as 'horse country' and the Saddlebred had his true foundations there, although for some time he was known as the Kentucky Saddler. These horses played a major part in the settlement of Ohio; they went south into Tennessee and across the Mississippi into Missouri. Missourians were proud of their equines and bred horses good enough to rival the Kentuckian originals. There is a saying: 'If Kentucky made the Saddle Horse, Missouri made him better.'

The horse recognized as the foundation sire was called Denmark, foaled in 1839. The Saddlebred found further fame in the American Civil War; at the end of the war, soldiers were allowed to keep their horses and Saddlebreds spread across the nation, taking with them the Denmark bloodlines.

The first American Saddlebred Horse Association was established at Louisville, Kentucky, in 1891, and Saddlebred horses can now be found in every State as well as in Canada, England, Germany, Holland, Scandinavia, Italy, Greece, Australia and Japan. In South Africa, the American Saddlebred is the most popular non-racing breed.

'If Kentucky made the Saddle Horse,
Missouri made him better.'

Spotted Saddle Horse

conformation attractive, straight head, long, sloping
    shoulders, short back, sloping hip, clean legs
colour all colourways and coat patterns
height 14.3–16 hands
uses riding, showing, utility

Prehistoric peoples etched their likeness on cave walls; Native Americans revered them as having magical powers – and as being ideally camouflaged for warhorses. Spotted horses have a long and proud history, and it was only a matter of time before the Americans bred a saddle horse with striking coat patterns. He was coveted for both his surefooted, comfortable ride as well as his beauty.

The New World's horses already had broken coats and spots, and many were also naturally gaited, a sign of their Spanish ancestry. Bred to bigger gaited horses, such as Morgans and Standardbreds, the little spotted ponies produced a pleasing light saddle horse – complete with spots and the comfortable gaits.

Latterly, Tennessee Walking Horse blood has been introduced, as has Mustang, Missouri Fox Trotter, Paso Fino and Peruvian Paso. The result is a striking, colourful equine with supreme gaits: the modern Spotted Saddle Horse can perform walk, trot, canter, rack, pace and fox trot. But the most important pace is the show gait, a fast walk that gives his rider the feeling he is gliding through the air propelled by a powerful but smooth-running machine.

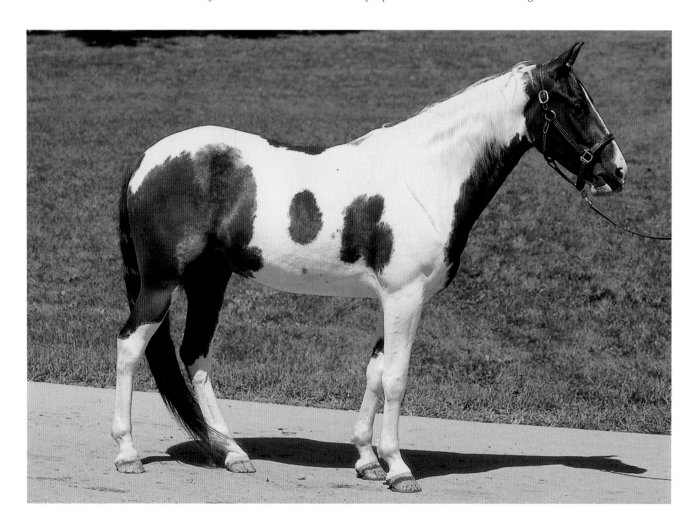

Standardbred

conformation refined head, medium-length neck, long
   back, muscular hindquarters, hindlegs set back
colour all solid colours
height 14–16 hands
uses racing, harness

The Standardbred is the world's fastest trotting horse and, although bred for speed rather than looks, still shows the Thoroughbred quality on which the breed is based. A Thoroughbred called Messenger, foaled in 1780, is given the credit for the breed – exported to America, he was bred to trotting mares, although he never raced himself. One of his grandsons, Hambletonian 10, was to sire some 1,335 progeny and 90 per cent of all modern Standardbreds trace back to him. He, too, never raced, but one of his sons, Dexter, set a trotting record of 1.6 km (1 mile) in 2 minutes 17 seconds.

The name Standardbred arose because the standard set for the early trotters was to cover a mile in less than three minutes. Almost every modern harness track is a mile long – but the first Standardbred races were contested on roads, owners challenging each other to see who had the swiftest horse. Streets in major cities were cleared so the races could take place, and many American towns still have a Race Street.

Pacing also gained popularity, with the first two-minute mile being recorded by a pacer called Star Pointer in 1897 – the record for a paced mile was set by Dan Patch, in 1 minute 55 seconds.

Campolina

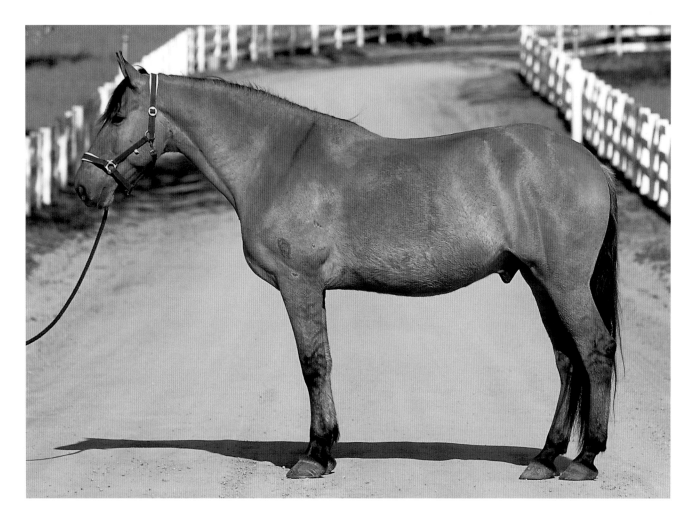

conformation convex profile, crested neck, powerful, compact body, strong legs, good feet
colour all colours
height 15–16.2 hands
uses riding, harness

Brazil is a country of music, and the Campolina makes a music all of his own, beating out a 'tacka tacka tacka' rhythm with his neat little feet. He takes his name from Cassiano Campolina, the Brazilian who first produced the breed at his Fazenda Tamque ranch near Buenos Aires.

Campolina began his horse-breeding operation in 1857, but it was a mare he acquired in 1870 that was to be the matriarch of the breed named for him. A black mare of Barb and Andalucian breeding called Medeia, she produced a dark grey colt called Monarca, who was to found the new breed, siring stock at the Fazenda Tamque for some 25 years.

Other stallions were used, among them Clydesdale, Holstein and American Saddlebred, the aim being to produce a horse of great beauty as well as supreme paces. His four-beat gait is known as the *marcha verdadair* (true march), which he can maintain at speeds of 9.6–12.8 kmph (6–8 mph).

The Campolina clearly shows his Spanish and Portuguese ancestry in his noble head and muscular stature. He possesses the flash and *brio* (arrogance and exuberance) of the Peruvian Paso, as well as the much-admired easy gait of the Mangalarga Marchador.

American Cream Draught

conformation convex profile, short, thick neck, compact body, short legs, some feather (leg hair)
colour medium cream, white mane and tail, pink skin and amber eyes, white markings
height 16.2 hands
uses harness, draught

America's only native draught horse breed is comparatively new, and its foundations lie with one mare, a light-coloured cream who passed her colour on to her progeny. Called Old Granny, she was thought to have been foaled between 1900 and 1905, and nothing is known of her breeding except that she was of heavy draught type – about 98 per cent of registered American Creams can be traced back to her.

A veterinary surgeon called Eric Christian was very taken by her cream foals and suggested to her owners, the Nelson brothers of Jewell, Iowa, that they keep a colt entire. The colt, Nelson's Buck, was the American Cream's foundation sire. Later, his great-grandson Silver Lace would also have considerable influence on the breed, despite standing as a stallion for only seven seasons before dying mysteriously in 1939, after an offer of $1,000 for him was turned down.

He was bred to various draught stock, including Belgian, Percheron and Shire, and continued to throw cream-coloured foals. In 1944, an association was established to perpetuate the breed and establish standards.

Interestingly, foals are born with almost white eyes, which darken when they reach a year old.

'foals are born with almost white eyes'

Ardennais

conformation large head, blunt nose, compact body, short back, short, stocky legs, short, full mane and tail
colour bay, roan, chestnut, grey, palomino
height 15.3–16.2 hands
uses draught

In this horse's massive head and stocky frame can be seen the coldblooded origins of his prehistoric ancestors. And, indeed, the Ardennais is one of the most ancient of draught breeds: he is descended from heavy horses praised by Julius Caesar in his commentaries on the Gallic Wars, and his ancestors are thought to have been bred in the Ardennes region of France, Belgium and Luxembourg for some 2,000 years, for both war and agriculture.

As a mountain type, the Ardennais is less heavy than his Belgian counterpart, but is still a sturdy, stocky equine of calm and sensible disposition. Despite his size, he is economical to keep and a tolerant and willing worker. During the French Revolution (1789–99), the Ardennais was considered to be the best artillery horse for his temperament, stamina and strength. In his disastrous campaign against Russia in 1812, Napoleon Bonaparte used Ardennais horses to transport heavy artillery and supplies. They were to perform much the same role in World War I.

In the 19th century, some Arab blood was introduced, and latterly Boulonnais, Percheron and the almost inevitable Thoroughbred. The modern Ardennais is an energetic, good-looking, chunky little horse – he is often said to be built like an equine tractor.

Auxois

conformation short head, muscular neck, prominent withers, wide, short back, hardy limbs
colour bay, roan, chestnut
height 16.3 hands and over
uses agriculture, forestry, light draught

Compact and powerful, the Auxois is closely related to the Ardennais, the result of crossings with local Burgundy mares and, later, with Boulonnais and Percheron, although since the early 20th century only Ardennais stallions have been used. A strong and enduring equine, he is thought to have existed side by side with the Ardennais since the Middle Ages and therefore, like the latter, is probably a descendant of the ancient Solutré Horse.

This horse is named for the lush Auxois area, which includes the southwest of Côte d'Or, an undulating, fertile region with rich pastures. He was originally smaller than the Ardennais, but has since overtaken his cousin in size. He has a short head with wide forehead, small, alert ears and a muscular, short neck. His wide chest and massive body give him the power to plough and, despite his bulk, he is supple and free-moving.

The Auxois is a quiet, good-natured and willing worker and this, coupled with his strength, makes him an excellent draught horse, suitable for farm work and forestry. But he has also found favour with the tourism industry, notably gypsy caravanning holidays in his beautiful homeland.

The Auxois has never been bred in large numbers, but this versatile draught horse has an increasing following.

Belgian Heavy Draught (Brabant)

conformation small, square head, heavily muscled neck, powerful shoulders, thick, compact body, short, strong legs
colour predominantly roan, also bay, chestnut, grey, dun
height 16.2–17 hands
uses heavy draught

A Goliath among heavy horses, the Belgian Heavy Draught owes his iron constitution and robust good health to the fertile land after which he is named. This lush little corner of Europe was home to the 'great horses' of war, the big black Flemish lines that were so revered by medieval warriors. Immensely strong and powerful, they could carry a knight in full armour with ease. Known for some centuries as the Flanders horse, he is also called the Brabant, for the area where he was bred, or *le Race de Trait Belge*.

The Belgian people were proud – and rightly so – of their draught breed and resisted the clamour for a lighter type of cavalry mount that was to follow, perpetuating the horse that so suited their country with its rich, heavy soil, as well as their climate, traditional skills and economic reliance on the land. Their glorious, powerful and versatile draught breed made up some 90 per cent of the country's equine population.

With what now seems like amazing foresight, the Belgians refused to dilute their heavy horse with outside blood, inbreeding selectively where necessary to develop further or preserve desired qualities, and adhering to strict breed guidelines.

By the 19th century, three distinct lines had been established, named for their founding sires. The Orange I line produced huge bay horses known as Gros de la Dendre, while the stallion Bayard established the Gris du Hainaut line of grey, dun or sorrel horses, with the occasional red roan, which reveals the breed's 'primitive' origins. The final line was founded by the bay Jean I – rather fancifully called Colosses de la Mehaigue – and was renowned for its strength and good, hard legs.

The Belgian Heavy Draught was almost universally popular and was used to form other heavy breeds, including the Shire and the Clydesdale. His fortunes continued, with many being exported – up until World War I, about 35,000 a year were sent to the United States, Canada and Russia, with America setting up her own breed association in 1887.

But inevitably the spread of mechanization affected the breed: the demand for draught horses went into serious decline and there were, at one time, less than 200 registered. The well-known brewery Coors is credited with saving the Belgian Heavy Draught – his traditional colour of glowing chestnut with white mane and tail is said to be reminiscent of a cold glass of beer with a head of foam.

'a glowing chestnut with white mane and tail is reminiscent of a cold glass of beer with a head of foam'

Black Forest Chestnut

conformation elegant head, muscular but refined neck, good shoulders, strong body, hard feet

colour sorrel to dark chestnut with blond/flaxen mane and tail

height 14.3–15.2 hands

uses agriculture, forestry, harness, riding, showing

In his German homeland, this horse is known as the Schwarzwalder Fuchs – the Black Forest Chestnut, 'pearl of the Black Forest'. He is an active, lively little horse, descended from the original coldblooded equines of the region, and the breed dates back some 600 years. The breed has been influenced by Noriker and Haflinger, whose colouring he has inherited, and made an excellent light draught horse to work the hilly region of the Black Forest in Baden-Wurttemberg, southwest Germany.

This horse is nimble and strong but has a gentle nature, and is versatile and willing. His colouring varies from sorrel through all shades of chestnut including a striking dark hue, spectacularly set off by a blond mane and tail. His good looks and happy disposition made him popular as an all-round family mount, as well as a farm horse. The studbook was established by the end of the 19th century, but efforts to encourage breeders to use Belgian Heavy Draughts to add height failed.

Today, there are about 46 state-approved stallions and approximately 700 registered mares in Germany. These numbers continue to grow as the popularity of the breed is once again on the rise.

Boulonnais

conformation fine head, arched neck, compact body, strong legs, light feather (leg hair), bushy mane
colour predominantly grey, sometimes black, occasionally chestnut
height 15–15.3 hands
uses draught

This breed's ancestors were the Numidian horses of war, brought by Julius Caesar's legions to the French coasts of Pas-de-Calais *en route* to invading Britain.

The Boulonnais is the Thoroughbred of all the heavy draught breeds, his beauty thought to be inherited from oriental and Andalucian blood brought into Belgium during the Crusades and Spanish occupation. It is these influences that set him apart from other draught horses. His speed, elegant build, refined head, silky coat and luxuriant mane can all be attributed to these hotblooded ancestors.

Energetic and lively, Boulonnais horses were as much in demand for riding as for pulling carriages and working the fields. In the 17th century, they were famed for pulling the fish carts to transport the fresh catch from the coast to Paris – this is now commemorated every other year in a traditional harness team race, 'la Route du Poisson'.

Modern Boulonnais Draughts are mostly grey of varying shades, although chestnut, dark bay and black have occurred. An attempt is being made to reintroduce the black colour, using a black stallion called Esope, and the modern breeding programme is government funded to save this superb draught breed from extinction.

Breton

conformation large head, straight profile, short, bulky neck, compact body, short, strong legs, small, hard feet
colour chestnut with flaxen mane and tail, bay, roan
height 14.3–16.3 hands
uses light or heavy draught

A demanding climate and less-than-fertile land shaped the Breton horse – named for Bretagne, or Brittany, in northwest France. Horses had been present in the region's mountains for thousands of years, although their provenance is open to debate, but this breed bears a resemblance to the Russian steppe horses. During the Crusades of the Middle Ages, the Breton was sought after by the military for his strength, stamina and comfortable gait, even though he stood only around 14 hands at that time. In the 17th century, Breton horses were exported to New France – Canada – by the French king.

As demand for types of horse changed, the Breton was crossed with other breeds including Boulonnais, Percheron and Ardennais. In the 19th century, Norfolk Trotter blood was introduced and resulted in the Postier Breton, which became the pride of the French Horse Artillery and was far more elegant than the original hairy little mountain horse. For his size, he had remarkably airy and easy gaits.

The Postier type is still found today, as is a heavier draught type, fast-maturing and sturdy, and possessing great strength and stamina and thus a valued work horse. The studbooks have been closed since 1920, ensuring the breed continues without dilution of foreign blood.

Dutch Heavy Draught

conformation straight profile, strongly muscled front, good withers, heavily muscled loins and hindquarters, good feet
colour chestnut, bay, roan, grey, black
height 16.3 hands
uses draught, agriculture

Like his close cousin the Belgian Heavy Draught, the Dutch version is a massive, powerfully built horse, but he can still show a lively turn of foot. He was developed in the Zeeland region of the Netherlands in the early 20th century specifically for working the sand and clay land of the country. Zeeland mares were bred to Belgian Heavy Draughts to produce an equine of great strength and stamina.

His popularity quickly grew, and the breed was found in large numbers throughout the provinces of Zeeland and north Brabant, where arable farms proliferated and where strong horses, that were also enduring and willing workers, were needed to plough the heavy marine clay and haul substantial loads across the farmland.

Like the Belgian, the Dutch Heavy Draught is an imposing, good-looking equine. Selective breeding has ensured he has strong, sound legs and feet. His profile is straight and he has small, mobile ears and a kind eye. He is an early-maturing horse who lives well into his twenties or even thirties, and despite his size he moves with a swinging, free gait.

While lesser horses may struggle in the heavy soil of his homeland, the Dutch Draught can almost skip over it – and he keeps going all day.

Clydesdale

conformation straight, broad head, long, thick neck, sloping shoulders, deep body, good feet
colour bay, brown, roan, black
height 17 hands and over
uses draught, harness, showing

He is the pride of Scotland, renowned for his size, weight and activity – the Clydesdale redefines the word 'horsepower'. The breed is influential but is comparatively new, beginning in the early 18th century when the 6th Duke of Hamilton imported Flemish stallions to Lanarkshire – the region used to be known as Clydesdale after the River Clyde, which runs through it. The Flemish blood was to improve existing horses and add size and power, and proved a great success.

The first stallion was dark brown, and the duke allowed his tenant farmers to use him on their mares free of charge. Then a John Paterson of Lochlyloch imported another Flemish stallion, black with a white face and some white on his legs. He was to prove highly influential on the development of the breed, and Lochlyloch blood became widely sought after.

An early feature of Scottish agriculture was the district system of hiring stallions to cover mares, which was not only successful but also meant records were kept, going back to 1837, and the Clydesdale became a standardized breed, with its own society being established in 1877.

The Clydesdale was bred not only to be of benefit to the farmers, but also to work in the coal industry and for all types of heavy haulage. His size and power soon gained recognition, and his reputation spread throughout Scotland and into northern England.

The handsome Clydesdale, for all his size and weight, is neither gross nor bulky and is a surprisingly active mover for so large a horse. His quality head, with its broad forehead and wide muzzle, is neither dished nor roman, and his arching neck is comparatively long for a draught breed. But it is his legs for which he is famed, and selective breeding has produced a horse with sound limbs with plenty of muscle and bone, and good (if rather flat) feet. He has a long, easy walk and springy, stylish trot.

The breed has been affected by changing times and changing emphasis – in the 1920s and 1930s, demand grew for a smaller, stockier type, while latterly a taller, leggier sort has become popular. Most worrying is the breed's status in the Rare Breeds Survival Trust. With ever-increasing mechanization during the 1960s and 1970s, Clydesdale numbers dwindled alarmingly and the breed was given 'vulnerable' status with the Trust; today, it is listed (more crucially) as 'at risk'.

What a tragedy it would be if this splendid equine giant disappeared altogether.

'the Clydesdale redefines the word "horsepower"'

Jutland

conformation plain, heavy head, short, thick neck, muscular shoulders, broad chest, short, strong legs
colour chestnut with flaxen mane and tail, black, brown
height 15–16 hands
uses draught

Denmark's heavy horse has been recorded on the Jutland peninsula since the Middle Ages, although it is thought he goes back further, perhaps to the time of the Vikings beginning in about the 9th century. Anglo-Saxon art depicts the Danish raiders rounding up prisoners astride powerful, compact horses that show remarkably similar characteristics to the modern Jutland.

He served in the 12th century as a sturdy warhorse – able to carry a knight in full armour with comparative ease – and later worked the fields of his native land. He is a strong, stocky equine, with a calm and kind disposition, and although his head is a little square with a tendency to plainness, he is far from unattractive.

Most Jutlands are chestnut with flaxen mane and tail – the chestnut colouring probably goes back to the English Suffolk Punch, which has had considerable influence on the modern breed. The Suffolk bloodlines are also evident in the horse's compact, round body, deep girth and enormous hindquarters, although, unlike the English breed, the Jutland has heavy feather (hair) on his lower legs, and brown or black horses do sometimes occur.

One of the greatest contributions to the Jutland in relatively recent times is that of a stallion called Oppenheimer. It is sometimes said he had Shire blood, but he was undoubtedly of Suffolk extraction. He was exported to Denmark from England in 1862. Some six generations later, a stallion called Oldrup Menkedal was born and was to become the recognized foundation sire of the breed, with almost all Jutlands today being traced back to two of his sons, Hovding and Prins af Jylland.

Danish Frederiksborg horses were also used on the Jutland to improve his paces, and later Cleveland Bay and Yorkshire Coach Horse blood was added, although this was not particularly successful. In turn, the Jutland is almost certainly the founding breed for the Schleswig Horse of northern Germany, which bears a strong resemblance to both the Jutland and the Suffolk Punch. Munkedal, a son of the stallion Oppenheimer, had considerable influence on the Schleswig.

Mechanization had a detrimental effect on the Jutland, but the Carlsberg Brewery traditionally used Jutlands to pull its drays – docile and willing, he is a tireless worker, easy to handle and economic to keep.

At one time, there were 210 Jutland horses with Carlsberg and today about 20 are still used for beer transportation in Copenhagen. The Carlsberg horses take part in many shows, festivals and films, promoting both the breed and the brewery.

'Anglo-Saxon art depicts Danish raiders rounding up prisoners astride horses remarkably similar to the modern Jutland.'

Latvian Draught

conformation straight profile, medium-length neck, strong
back, deep girth, good legs
colour bay, brown, black, chestnut
height 15.2–16 hands
uses harness, draught, riding, competition

When the Republic of Latvia was founded in 1918, a great effort was made to register and improve the country's horse breed, which probably had its ancestry in the Tarpan. There was a significant lack of horses in Latvia after World War I, so Oldenburgs, Hanoverians and Holsteins were imported for crossing with the local stock.

The Okte Stud, which was to become the cradle for the breed, was founded in 1921, and between then and 1940, 65 Oldenburg stallions and 42 mares were imported from the Netherlands and Germany to form the core of the Latvian Draught. As well as purebred Oldenburgs, Oldenburg crosses and Hanoverians, Norfolk Roadsters, Ardennais and East Friesians were also widely used. The warmblood breeding contributed to the breed's overall good looks and sensible nature.

In 1925, a state-owned Svetciems stud farm was opened, where mares owned by the army and proven in sports were used. Two types of Latvian, the harness horse and the sports version, have since evolved. Since 1960 the popularity of equestrian sports has shifted the breeding focus. The harness type is a big, strong utility horse, while the sports horse has enjoyed worldwide success. The dressage horse Rusty, competed by Ulla Salzgeber, is of Latvian breeding.

Murakozi

conformation large, convex head, well-defined withers, compact body, low-set tail, short, strong legs
colour liver chestnut with flaxen mane and tail, brown, grey, black, bay
height 16 hands
uses draught

Hungary's heavy horse originated in the late 19th and early 20th centuries around the River Mura region in the southern part of the country, as a strong and fast draught breed.

Native Hungarian mares, known as Mur-Insulan – meaning 'confined to the Mura region' – were crossed with Ardennais, Norikers and Percherons, as well as with Hungarian half-breds that contained Thoroughbred and Arab blood. The result was an exceptionally strong and active draught horse, standing about 16 hands and ideal for heavy farm work. He was good-looking as well as good-tempered, and was noted for being sound, reliable and economic to keep. This made him the mount of choice for the army.

Following World War I, there was a rapid increase in arable farming in central and eastern Europe, and the active Murakozi was much in demand. In the early 20th century the breed flourished, with an estimated one in five horses in Hungary being a Murakozi. A great many were lost in World War II, but in the late 1940s efforts were made to revitalize the breed, using Ardennais stallions. However, the decline in demand from the agricultural industry means he is unlikely to regain his earlier popularity.

'an exceptionally strong, fast and active draught horse'

Normandy Cob

conformation large head, medium length of rein, powerful,
    stocky frame, short, muscular legs, sound feet
colour chestnut, bay, roan
height 15.3–16.2 hands
uses light draught, riding

Since the 10th century, Normandy has been renowned as
excellent horse-breeding country, its limestone subsoil and
lush pasture providing an ideal 'nursery' for rearing equines.
The Normandy Cob descended from native horses, known as
bidets, in existence since before Roman times. Tough and
enduring, these equines were probably brought to France
from Asia by the Celts and, as well as Mongolian influences,
there would have been refining Eastern blood in the mix.

The Romans crossed the *bidets* with their heavier pack
mares to produce a strong utility horse. Later, in the 16th and
17th centuries, Arab and Barb blood was added, followed by
Thoroughbred and Norfolk Roadster.

The royal stud at Saint-Lô, in the La Manche region of
Normandy, was founded in 1806, and Normandy Cobs were
also bred at Le Pin. Their name was prompted by the English
all-round cob type of horse.

Two distinct types were bred: the heavyweight riding
horse for the cavalry and a sturdier, stockier sort for draught
work – today, the breed is still used in agriculture. The
draught horses were traditionally docked, as it was thought
the full tail of a horse in harness could become dangerously
entangled with the reins. Docking is now prohibited in some
countries and tails are plaited and bound instead.

Percheron

conformation fine head, long neck, deep chest, short back, sound, clean limbs
colour grey, black
height 14.3–16.1 hands
uses light draught, harness, riding

An ancient breed, the Percheron's ancestors were Arab horses brought to La Perche in Normandy, France, by the invading Moors defeated at the Battle of Tours in AD 732. Their abandoned steeds were bred to existing heavy Flemish stock to produce the Percheron horse. During the Crusades, more Arab blood was added, and the resulting equine was widely recognized as an outstanding warhorse of great beauty, as well as substance and soundness.

By the 17th century, the breed was in great demand – France's heavy mail coaches were traditionally pulled by Percheron horses. In the 19th century, breeders at the royal stud at Le Pin introduced two Arab stallions. One, Gallipoli, sired a horse called Jean Le Blanc in 1823, and all today's Percheron bloodlines trace back to him.

Later, more Arab blood was introduced to add flash and fire, and the modern Percheron is perhaps the most elegant of all draught breeds – but although spirited, he still has a kind disposition. He makes a good riding horse and, crossed with Thoroughbred or warmblood, produces an excellent competition horse.

Only Percherons bred in La Perche may be entered in the studbook – those bred outside have a separate studbook – ensuring this wonderful breed stays pure.

Poitevin (Mullasier)

conformation heavy head, straight shoulders, sloping
  crop, heavy feather (leg hair), large, flat feet
colour dun, roan, bay, black, grey
height 16–16.2 hands
uses mule production

Almost unknown outside its native France, the Poitevin or Mullasier was mostly used for breeding mules when crossed with the Poitou donkeys that inhabited the same region – perhaps brought by the Romans, who also bred mules.

The Poitevin is thought to be a descendant of Flemish horses brought to Marais Poitou in the 17th century to drain the marshland, which were related to both the Clydesdale and the Shire, as well as Dutch, Danish and Norwegian stock.

When crossed with the local donkeys, the Poitevin produced an exceptionally large and strong mule, said to be the finest working mule in the world. These animals fetched high prices, and it has been estimated that at the height of the industry – around the turn of the 19th/20th centuries – the Poitou region was producing some 30,000 mules a year.

The Poitevin himself is somewhat unprepossessing, with a heavy head, thick mane and tail, and abundant coarse feather, and he is rather slow-moving, which makes him less popular than other heavy breeds for draught work.

With the decline in demand for mules following World War II, the breed is now perilously close to extinction, with little call for its continuation. There are thought to be only about 300 Poitevins left, although efforts are being made to revive the breed.

Russian Heavy Draught

conformation straight or slightly convex profile, medium-length neck, deep chest, long back, short, powerful legs
colour mostly chestnut or roan
height 14.3 hands
uses light draught, agriculture

Russia once had more horses per head of population than any other European country apart from Iceland. Her heavy draught was recognized as a breed only in 1952, although he began his evolution in the late 19th century.

Local horses, vital for farm work, were improved using Orlov Trotter, Percheron and Ardennais blood. The latter breed, introduced to Russia in the 1880s, was to prove particularly influential on the country's draught horse, in both temperament and conformation – in the 1920s, the breed was known as the Russian Ardennes. In 1875, there were nine Ardennes stallions in Russia; by 1915, there were 597.

The Russian Heavy Draught is a good, willing worker that matures early, achieving his full height usually within 18 months, and he is an economic keeper – but the horse was not valued for his agricultural suitability alone. The breed is noted for its milk-producing ability: fermented mares' milk – *kymus* – was believed to be an exceptionally beneficial tonic and was championed by the literary greats of the 19th century, among them Alexander Pushkin and Leo Tolstoy. The milk was thought to stimulate the appetite, improve digestion and increase immunity to disease, and was recommended variously for conditions such as gastritis, anaemia, tuberculosis and impotence.

Shire

conformation large convex head, long neck, wide chest, muscular body, long, heavy legs, good bone
colour black, bay, brown, grey, with white markings
height 18 hands and over
uses heavy draught, showing

William the Conqueror brought the renowned medieval 'great horse' to Britain in the 11th century following the Norman Conquest, where he served as an equine form of armoured tank, his great size and strength allowing him to carry a fully armoured knight with ease.

The breed was improved using Flemish and Belgian stallions and Friesian blood – for a time, he was known as the English Black, until other influences made this a misnomer.

Improved further by the renowned breeder Robert Bakewell in the 18th century, he was also for a while known as the Bakewell Black.

By the time the breed society was founded in 1878, the 'black' part of his name was no longer appropriate, as he was now found in an abundance of colours including bay, brown and grey, with white markings.

The name Shire comes from the Saxon *schyran* (divide), with many English Midlands counties being known as shires. King Henry VIII is said to have coined the name Shire Horse in the 16th century.

This gentle equine giant is still popular, with classes for ridden purebreds and partbreds having been introduced at English shows. The Shire Horse has become synonymous with strength, constitution, energy and endurance.

Suffolk Punch

conformation intelligent head, powerful, arched neck, short, strong back, level croup, short legs

colour bright, red, golden, yellow, light, dark and dull dark chesnut*

height 16.1–17.1 hands

uses light draught, harness, riding, showing

This is one of the oldest draught horse breeds, whose foundation sire, Crisp's Horse of Ufford, Suffolk (in the East Anglia region), was foaled in 1768, although the breed was described as early as the 15th century. He is always chesnut – *traditionally spelt without the middle 't' – in seven recognized shades: bright, red, golden, yellow, light, dark and dull dark.

He has a fine, intelligent head with neat, short ears and a kind eye; his muscular neck is well arched and he is compact and short-coupled. His legs are rather short and this gives the impression that his body is too big for them. This shape gives the Suffolk its nickname 'Suffolk Punch', as well as its great strength. There is no height limit.

Short they may be, but this horse's legs are clean and strong, with no feather (leg hair), ideal for working the heavy clay soil of the Suffolk farms for which he was developed. Docile and hardworking, the Suffolk Punch is sound and long-lived, and the isolation in which he was bred has led to an unusually uniform and pure breed.

Good feet are highly prized in this breed, and foot classes are still held at East Anglian shows, where it is the horse's foot and not the standard of shoeing that is judged.

Italian Heavy Draught (Tiro Pesante Rapido)

conformation small, square head, arched neck, strong
    back, short legs, good feet
colour predominantly chestnut, also bay, roan
height 15–16 hands
uses draught

Italy's heavy horse is renowned for his rapid trot, which he can keep up for some distance even while pulling a heavy cart. He is sometimes called Tiro Pesante Rapido, which means 'quick heavy draught'.

The breed was developed in northern Italy in the 19th and 20th centuries, when the Italians sought to improve their existing equine stock. Experiments with imported Belgian Heavy Draught horses proved only partially successful – the resulting offspring were certainly better than the native stock, but were still too heavy and slow for Italian farm work. Further outcrosses with Percheron and Boulonnais went some way to producing the required type – and the latter passed on his swift, active trot – but it wasn't until some Breton blood was added in the 1920s, that the new breed really began to evolve.

The Italian Heavy Draught is an attractive little horse with a kind and docile nature. Most are chestnut with flaxen mane and tail, or roan, although bays do sometimes occur. He has a hardy constitution, is economical to keep and matures early – another point in his favour.

In his native land, where he is used for farm work, he is very popular – about a third of all breeding stallions in Italy are the country's native heavy horse.

Vladimir Heavy Draught

conformation clean head, long, well-muscled neck, pronounced withers, long back, long legs
colour mostly bay, black, brown
height 16.1 hands
uses draught, harness

Clydesdale and Shire horses exerted considerable influence on the Vladimir Heavy Draught, considerable numbers of both breeds being exported to Russia at the end of the 19th century. He was originally developed in the Ivanovo and Vladimir provinces, taking his name from the latter. There were around 20 Russian studs breeding Clydesdales in the early 20th century, with stallions including Lord James, Border Brand and Glen Albin having significant influence.

Officially recognized in 1946, the breed is tall and well proportioned, although less easy-going than other draught horses. But he is undeniably striking – and looks stupendous in harness – with longer and lighter legs than most heavy horses, and freer action. The Vladimir Heavy Draught is strong and can pull heavy loads at speed – he is renowned for his nimble gaits.

He undoubtedly owes his legginess to his Clydesdale roots, the Shire influences being less dominant. Some Percheron and Suffolk Punch blood was added later, as was Cleveland Bay, but by the 1920s there were a sufficient number of crossbreds to form the foundation Vladimir herd.

Less than 30 years ago there were some 2,300 Vladimirs, but numbers have since declined and Clydesdale and Shire stallions have recently been imported to save the breed.

Irish Draught

conformation attractive head, carried high on well-set neck, clean shoulders, powerful back, good, sound legs
colour all solid colours
height 15.2–17 hands
uses hunting, competition, riding, showing

He is the horse of warriors, a mighty steed that has carried man into battle for centuries – the *Cuchulain Saga*, written in 1 BC, describes a powerful chariot horse of Irish Draught type.

The Anglo-Normans arrived in Ireland in the 12th century, bringing with them their robust warhorses, which were bred to native Irish stock. In the 16th century, trade between southern Ireland and Spain brought Spanish blood into the mix. As his reputation as a warhorse grew, the Irish Draught was subsequently exported in great numbers to armies throughout Europe, and during World War I he served on the front line in his thousands.

In his native land, the Irish Draught was a farm horse, working on the Irish smallholdings, transporting the farmer and his family to church in a trap or dogcart, and taking the farmer hunting. He was also economical to keep – a boon for struggling farmers – as his traditional winter feed was chopped young gorse, boiled turnips and bran or meal that could be spared from the cows. The horse possesses an exuberant natural jump and can cover the ground at a smooth, unflagging gallop. Indeed, crossing the Irish Draught with the Thoroughbred results in the world-renowned Irish hunter, now known as the Irish Sport Horse, which excels not just at hunting but in every equestrian discipline and which is in considerable demand.

Energetic and graceful, the Irish Draught evolved into a quality horse, with a big, kind eye, attractive head, powerful body, short, strong legs and excellent hard feet. One reason the Irish Draught is so in demand for breeding show jumpers is the durability of his feet. Despite the 'draught' part of his name, he is in no way coarse but is an all-round good-looking equine, free-moving and active. Yet for all his great power, he is docile and kind.

The great Irish famine of 1845–9 caused a significant reduction in the number of Irish Draughts, and agricultural recessions in the 1870s added to the breed's decline. As the economy improved, demand for horses increased, and English breeds such as the Clydesdale were imported, which were subsequently bred with the existing Irish Draughts to produce a bigger, slightly coarser type. To keep the traditional breed alive, the first studbook was opened in 1917, with 375 mares and 44 stallions.

As mechanization changed the shape of the agricultural industry, its Irish workhorse was brought to the brink of extinction. The Irish Draught Horse Society was established in 1976 with the sole aim of saving the breed. Today, the breed's fortunes are again on the rise, with Irish Draught Horse Societies founded in Britain, the United States and Canada, Australia and New Zealand.

'he is the horse of warriors, a mighty steed that has carried man into battle for centuries'

Hunter

conformation varies
colour varies
height 15.2–17 hands
uses hunting

Arguably, the best hunter is the result of crossing the pure-bred Irish Draught with the English Thoroughbred, producing a sound, powerful horse that can keep going all day and take any obstacle in his stride. But the hunter is a type, rather than a breed, and the only requirements are that he can jump and gallop.

Hunting as a sport began in England in the 15th century, when the landed gentry would hunt deer, the fox being viewed as an inferior creature. Modern foxhunting is attributed to one Hugo Meynell, who perfected the art of crossing the country at speed more than 300 years ago. Foxhunting caught on in a big way and there were soon foxhound packs in every corner of Britain and Ireland. In 2005, traditional hunting with hounds was banned in England and Wales.

The type of horse needed varied according to the terrain he would have to cross, but the Irish hunter was almost universally popular, with his innate ability to 'find an extra leg' over fences and get himself out of trouble. With the growth of popularity in hunting in the United States, where they hunt red and grey fox as well as coyote, English and Irish hunters are both popular – the more Thoroughbred blood, the more strength, speed and scope. However, perhaps the most important quality for the hunter is courage.

Brumby

conformation no standardized type
colour all colours
height 14–15 hands
uses feral

Australia's feral horse is not indigenous to the continent, but is the descendant of stock brought over by the settlers in the 18th and 19th centuries. These horses were of Thoroughbred and draught stock and only the fittest survived the gruelling journey to their new land.

There is some debate over the origins of the breed's name. A James Brumby, originally from Lincolnshire in England, arrived in Australia in 1791. He was a soldier with the New South Wales Corp and he was also a farrier, perhaps with responsibility for the horses of the new colony. He moved to Tasmania in 1804 and it is thought that he left some horses in New South Wales. When locals asked who owned the horses, they were told 'they're Brumby's'.

Sadly, the modern Brumby is seen as more of a pest than a resource, although his mane and tail hair is used for musical instruments, brushes and upholstery. Brumbies are too wild to be of much practical use as riding or stock horses, and are often inferior specimens, somewhat unprepossessing to say the least. The feral herds also damage fences, overgraze cattle pastures, drink and foul water supplies, and make cattle mustering more difficult. For their own health, the Brumby herds are frequently humanely culled.

Camargue

conformation large, plain head, short neck, upright
   shoulders, thickset body, short, well-formed legs
colour grey
height 13–14 hands
uses riding

France's 'horse of the sea' roams wild in the Rhône delta, in what is now the Camargue National Park. He is one of the world's oldest horse breeds, believed to be a descendant of the now extinct Solutré horse, which lived in the marshy lands of the region near the sea. Skeletal remains of the Solutré, dating from the palaeolithic period 17,000 years ago, are almost identical to the Camargue.

The Camargue would almost certainly have been influenced by early stock being brought through the region by various raiders, including Greeks, Romans and Arabs – conversely, it is thought the Camargue had some influence on Spanish breeds, as returning armies took them home.

He is an exceptionally hardy creature; there is little to nourish him in the vast swampland that is his home, where the notorious Mistral blows cold across the delta. He is always grey, the foals being born dark brown or black and lightening through all shades of grey to white as they mature.

The Camargue is now protected, with annual round-ups to brand fillies and geld any colts or stallions unsuitable for breeding. Lively, agile and brave, the horses are broken to saddle to round up the black bulls of the region.

Chincoteague

conformation neat head, medium-length neck, short back, rounded hindquarters, low-set tail
colour all colours
height 13–14.2 hands
uses riding

Legend has it that the feral ponies that live on the islands of Assateague and Chincoteague off the coast of Virginia and Maryland are descendants of stock that swam to shore from a wrecked Spanish galleon. The more likely explanation for this hardy breed's existence is that they were brought to the islands by settlers.

The ponies were made famous by Marguerite Henry's much-loved book *Misty of Chincoteague*, based on a true story, and the breed is named for the smaller island separated from Assateague by a narrow channel – Chincoteague means 'beautiful land across water'.

Today, there are two herds on Assateague, one on the Virginia end of the island and one on the Maryland end. The former is managed by the Chincoteague Volunteer Fire Company, the latter by the National Park Service.

The Virginia herd is rounded up by 'saltwater cowboys' each July, and at slack tide is swum across the channel to Chincoteague in front of thousands of cheering spectators. Foals are auctioned off and the remaining horses swum back to Assateague the following day. The ponies make excellent children's rides, being both intelligent and willing. They are exceptionally hardy and economic to keep – it is said of the Chincoteague that he 'can get fat standing on concrete'.

Mustang

conformation intelligent head, medium-length neck
 and back, clean legs, small, hard feet
colour all colours
height 13–15 hands
uses riding, ranching, rodeo, pleasure riding, endurance

His name means 'ownerless horse' and he is the descendant of the Spanish horses – a mixture of Barb, Arab, Sorraia and Andalucian blood brought over by the Spanish conquistadors. Native horses that inhabited the North American continent became extinct about 10,000 years ago, and the Native Americans had never before seen such creatures. Under Spanish rule, the Native Americans were not allowed to own horses, but during the revolt in 1680 the Spaniards beat a hasty retreat and left their horses behind.

The Native Americans soon learned to ride, and this ability transformed them from plodding pedestrians into nomadic hunters and warriors, with cultures wholly dependent upon horses. They spread across the Great Plains, hunting only the best game, and their horses were highly valued. The tribe medicine man would say prayers over the warriors' horses before a big battle or buffalo hunt; a handprint, dots or zigzags would be marked on the legs or rump, or circles drawn around the horse's eyes. The prized warhorses were decorated extravagantly with ribbons, feathers and plaits, and it was also customary to split one or both ears.

The wild herds of Mustang were formed of horses that escaped from the Native American tribes or from ranchers, who would release their horses to fend for themselves during the winter, and recapture them when needed in the spring. The feral herds bred unchecked, with an estimated two million or more by 1900. By this time they were viewed as a nuisance, competing with cattle for grazing and water. Ranchers would shoot the wild horses indiscriminately and numbers were drastically reduced, with fewer than 17,000 remaining by 1970.

Stating that Mustangs were 'living symbols of the historic and pioneer spirit of the West', the United States Congress passed the Wild Free-Roaming Horse and Burro Act in 1971 to protect the feral herds, and an estimated 41,000 mustangs roam wild today. Shooting or poisoning the horses is illegal, and the penalties for doing so are severe.

However, contrary to belief, the Mustang is tameable, and possesses an innate 'cow sense' that makes him ideal for ranching, while his agility and energy make him a good all-rounder. He can be found all over the United States as a pleasure horse, and his stamina – no doubt the product of centuries of natural selection – means he is a good endurance ride. While he has contributed to the formation of many American breeds – Morgan, Quarter Horse, Saddlebred, Tennessee Walker, Appaloosa and Buckskin – the Mustang himself remains largely unchanged.

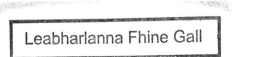

INDEX

Acknowledgements

Executive Editor Trevor Davies
Editor Charlotte Wilson
Executive Art Editor Leigh Jones
Designer Colin Goody
Senior Production Controller Manjit Sihra
Picture Researcher Sophie Delpech
Photographer Bob Langrish
Artwork Cactus Design and Illustration

Picture Acknowledgements
Main Photography © Bob Langrish
Other Photography Frank Lane Picture Agency/
Frans Lanting 12 bottom left.
Photolibrary Group/IFA-Bilderteam GMBH 11.